MY NAME IS ANGEL

MY NAME IS ANGEL

Rhea Coombs with Diane Taylor

This paperback edition first published in 2007 by
Virgin Books Ltd
Thames Wharf Studios
Rainville Road
London
W6 9HA

First published in Great Britain in paperback in 2007 by
Virgin Books Ltd
First published in Great Britain in hardback in 2007 by
Virgin Books Ltd

A catalogue record for this book is available from
the British Library.

ISBN 978 0 7535 1944 8

The paper used in this book is a natural, recyclable product
made from wood grown in sustainable forests. The
manufacturing process conforms to the regulations of the
country of origin.

Typeset by TW Typesetting, Plymouth, Devon

Printed and bound in Great Britain by
CPI Bookmarque, Croydon

1 3 5 7 9 10 8 6 4 2

For my children;
for the women on the street

CONTENTS

FOREWORD

M*y Name is Angel* is the story of a girl who desperately wanted to fit in but somehow didn't. Her mother was a free spirited young woman who travelled across Europe with Rhea, feeding her vegan fare while she craved white socks in suburbia and meat and two veg.

At the age of fourteen she discovered drugs and danger and the anaesthetising properties of taking reckless risks. For a while she felt a part of the disparate group of Yardies, addicts and other miscellaneous people from the world of unbelonging. She had two young children by the time she was in her early twenties but as the parallel universe of drugs and prostitution seeped into her soul she gave them up, entrusting them to the father of her second child.

She joined London's underworld, working as a hostess in a Soho clip joint. Later she paced the streets of south London for punters who would give her the £20 she needed for her next fix of 'brown and white' – crack and heroin. More fearless than many women involved in drugs and prostitution, she spent days and nights in crack houses with hardened gangsters who guarded their mountains of crack and cash with state-of-the-art handguns. One of these gangsters decided she had businesswoman potential and put her in charge of his crack house. It is virtually unheard of for a woman to occupy such a position in the patriarchal world of crack houses but she succeeded, sweeping the floor and bleaching the sink in between handing out little white rocks of crack.

After a while the drugs which had once given her such an overwhelming sense of belonging stopped working. She decided that life with the dealers, gangsters, addicts and assorted lost souls who inhabit London's underworld wasn't the balm she had once thought it was. Every day she yearned for her children. She decided that the only way she would ever hold them in her arms again and hear about their day at school was by employing some superhuman effort of will. She walked away from the drugs, the prostitution and the gangsters, got her children back and at the age of 33 has discovered what pure joy feels like. She has a real job for the first time in her life, working for a church-based charity helping women like herself leave prostitution. She has travelled the long way round to achieve the normal life she craves but she has arrived and she is determined to stay.

PROLOGUE

I t was just after 9 p.m. on New Year's Eve, 2002, when the worst possible thing happened. I saw my son.

I was standing, with teeth chattering, on the pavement on New Park Road in Streatham. Ridiculous illuminated Santas installed by the council swung from the street lights. Revellers staggered out of one pub and into the next, singing loud, tuneless football anthems. The silhouettes of warm, purposeful drivers bled into one another as their cars hummed past me. I prayed one would stop, wind down his window and say the magic words: 'Doin' business tonight, love?' The warm fuzz of the heroin I'd injected a few hours before was beginning to fade. I knew I couldn't wait too long to earn money for my next hit.

A car did slow down and stopped when it was almost parallel with my ankles. At first my heart leapt. I hoped that the driver was a generous man and that his car would be nice and warm with a clean, dry, back seat. Given that it was the festive season I calculated that I might earn £40 instead of my usual £20. I smiled an expectant work smile, one that hid my teeth, didn't crease my lipstick and didn't reach my eyes. He opened the car door instead of doing the standard negotiation at the wheel and suddenly the pink flush of anticipation I'd felt a few seconds ago was doused by the coldest of sweats.

The man wasn't a punter but my old friend Karen's partner Patrick, and sitting in the back of the car with his children, laughing and joking, was my son Paul. I was lost to my beloved son yet here I was, standing, gasping in the jeans I'd made diagonal slashes through to reveal the fishnet tights underneath and a long, dark plastic coat I thought I looked dramatic in. He was laughing with the other children. I glimpsed his gap-toothed grin I ached to see every day. He was so absorbed in his conversation that he didn't incline his head in my direction. We had been through everything together, Paul and me. I'd run with him from his violent father when he was just a few months old, I'd carried him on my back down a drainpipe when we escaped from another violent lover. He had watched without understanding my descent into what began as a love affair with speed and ecstasy and spiralled into the most abusive relationship of all with the crack pipe I hid under the floorboards of our home. Yet through it all he had offered me pure, unsullied, unconditional love. I had failed him. I could no longer bear him to see me gripped tighter and tighter by the drugs and by the chaotic, violent lifestyle that financed them. I thought that unless I placed him firmly outside the crazed sphere I inhabited he would become horribly tainted by it, morally disfigured. So I gave him up. Darren, the father of my younger daughter Keira, agreed to take both her and Paul until I could sort myself out.

But the shame of letting down my children and losing them made me use more drugs, toss away the boundaries I had imposed on myself when I had them to look after and allow myself to drift into the centre of the deepest, darkest sea on a scum-powered wave. Without my children there was nothing left and preserving my life seemed pointless.

In another split second Paul would turn towards me. And then his beautiful grin would freeze on his face to be replaced by anger, hurt and confusion. Darren and I had told the children that I was ill and that I needed to go to hospital to make me better. That was several months ago and I hadn't seen them at all in that time.

I felt I had no choice. I started to run. There was a small side street and I darted into it, squeezing myself flat under the belly of a car that dripped oil through the slashes of my jeans and the holes in my fishnets on to my chilled skin. I waited for ten minutes and then crawled out and started running again. Perhaps it was crack-induced paranoia or perhaps Patrick really was driving around the same few streets looking for me. He had been about to say, 'Hi, how are you, what are you up to?', but I couldn't bear to hear those words.

In my bag the miscellaneous lighters, the miniature brandy bottle I'd converted into a crack pipe and a handful of long, orange needles to inject deliciously numbing heroin banged against my thigh as I ran.

I sprinted for a hundred yards and then hid again, this time behind a bush. I took out of my jacket pocket a small pearl-handled knife I had stolen from a crack house a few weeks before. I told myself I could use it against any punter who became violent although I never had. Just knowing that it nestled in my pocket and running my thumb rhythmically up and down the polished handle comforted me.

As I crouched and trembled, the usual feelings of remorse and self-loathing flooded my stomach so full that I thought I was going to vomit green bile of shame. But for the first time I felt something else as well. A sense of resolve, which can only begin to flicker when the most absolute despair has been reached. I vowed that somehow I would lift myself out of my mire, cast aside all the sham comforts of narcotics and once again hold my children in my arms.

1. THE HIPPY CHILD

My mother couldn't stand life in suburbia. She had grown up in a nice house in a nice street in a nice part of south London in the 1950s. Her parents obeyed the rules of the time. Her father clipped the privet hedge every weekend during the summer months while her mother polished the front step until it shone and impressed the neighbours with the display of dazzling whites which she pegged out onto the washing line in the back garden more regularly than anyone else in the street.

By the time my mother became a teenager and understood that rebellion was a possibility, The Beatles had embraced love and peace. My mother couldn't understand how her parents could be happy pinioned to the same four walls for ever. And so as soon as she could, she fluttered out of the cage and became a free agent. With her long hair streaming down her back, her ankle-length gypsy skirt and her wristful of jangling bangles, she walked out on suburbia. She took up with a series of boyfriends her parents disapproved of and started travelling across Europe to music festivals. After the stifling, prim environment of her childhood, my mother became the proverbial kid let loose in the sweet shop. She got pregnant with my brother Tony at the age of seventeen. Her parents insisted on a speedy wedding. The union crumbled soon after they walked down the aisle.

All I know about my father is that he had a drink problem and that he murdered a gay man by stamping on his face. I've never known much about how they met, whether their relationship was initially harmonious or not or how he felt about me. He and my mother split up when I was about one but I do have one very early memory of him. We were at my grandmother's house when I was about six months old. He was standing in an upstairs room holding me in his arms and I was looking out of the window. I don't remember feeling scared as he held me and the memory is not an unpleasant one. I've never met my father although I do wonder from time to time what it would be like to see the person who gave me the other 50 per cent of my genes. Do I look like him? Have I inherited any of his personality traits? Did he pass the addiction gene on to me if such a thing exists? I have no answers – that part of my personal history is a blank page.

My mother decided to keep me with her on her travels. She gave birth to me in Plymouth but moved soon afterwards to a flat in London. My earliest memory, at the age of three, is of my mother's often disastrous attempts to make elderberry wine. We were living in a place in Balham, south London, and she constructed an elaborate jumble of bubbling pots and tubes to transform the innocent elderflowers into something inebriating. Occasionally it worked and my mother and her friends glugged the liquid from chipped mugs, toasting nature's riches. More often, though, the homemade brewing contraption exploded, leaving reproachful elderflower stains on the kitchen ceiling.

'Ah well, we'll have to go out picking elderflowers again tomorrow, won't we, Rhea?' she said.

For a while I was happy in the flat. A family of five children lived in the basement and my mother often left me with them overnight. All the children tumbled into the available beds together. At first I loved the companionship of the other children. I saw my older brother irregularly and my identity was that of an only child. But one night, one of the boys in the family who I was lying next to in bed started touching me. I didn't understand what he was doing, or that it was wrong. All I knew was that I felt scared and that he had punctured the happiness I felt with him and his sisters and brothers. After that I tried to keep away from him. I wasn't old enough to articulate to my mother what had happened to me that night but often I begged her to take me with her when she went out instead of leaving me with the basement family.

In those early years my ears were filled with the sounds of The Beatles, Jimi Hendrix and black roots music. While my mother cooked a seemingly endless variety of lentil-based dishes, fiddled with her elderberry wine equipment, tended her lemon balm and spider plants or lounged on floor cushions, this music always played.

The noise of the music and the crowd of chattering Bohemians who streamed through my mother's front door encouraged me to fall silent. It seemed too hard to make myself heard over the insistent bass lines and babble of voices so I gave up and occupied myself by becoming an observer. My mother often seemed absorbed in her latest boyfriend so I tried to entertain myself.

She sent me to the local primary school but in my hippy waistcoats and brown dungarees I felt painfully isolated from the popular girls in their pristine knee-high white socks and polished black patent shoes.

One of those girls, Anna, who seemed to be cherished by both teachers and children alike, fingered the strap of my dungarees one day, wrinkled her nose with distaste and said, 'Your clothes are weird, Rhea,' before walking off giggling with a group of girls who looked like her and dressed like her.

I retreated increasingly at school. My chin was slumped almost permanently against my chest in the hope of avoiding adverse comments from heartless children. But while I withdrew from my peers, I yearned to be accepted by them. And even the mildest rejection felt like a frenzied stab wound to the stomach.

The pain that shredded my insides most of all was my mother's failure to deliver me to and collect me from school at the right times. She sometimes dropped me off half an hour late, something that I as a four-year-old was inexplicably blamed for by my teachers. And she sometimes collected me half an hour late in the afternoons. On those occassions I stood expectantly in the playground watching the other mothers run up to their offspring and envelop them in a big, secure hug. I prayed that my mother would appear before the playground was entirely empty but she rarely did. I dreamed of showing off to the other children that I too had a mother who played by the rules of parenthood. Sometimes the teachers would take me brusquely by the hand and plonk me in a corner at the after-school club. I was not particularly welcome there because I hadn't been booked in. I was a spare part that no one quite knew what to do with. Those days that I stood in the playground or cowered at the after-school club I dreamed of being dead or of being able to do the kind of magic which could whisk me far away from the earthly horrors of school or at the very least make me an invisible presence in the playground. As I stood awkwardly behind the metal front gates, I stared down at my arms and legs and stomach, hating the fact that they existed and made me noticeable. I wished very hard that I was no longer solid, material Rhea but instead a weightless fairy woven out of invisible gossamer thread.

From the moment I began having conscious thought processes I was aware of a fundamental mismatch between my body and my soul. I had a child's sense of God as the man in the sky with all the answers and I often cast my eyes heavenwards asking perplexedly: 'Why have you put me on the earth?' I felt guilty about things that were not my fault like the explosions of my mother's elderberry wine. I thought that if I'd tiptoed a bit more quietly around our flat the wine would have remained safely inside the container. When I suffered in the school playground I felt as if I was being punished for something but I had no idea what it could be. All the other children around me seemed happy. Their insides and outsides seemed to be at one like a two-piece jigsaw puzzle. I presumed that because I didn't feel the way they did I had been put on earth by mistake. I wondered and wondered why I had been born. Later as I edged towards adolescence these feelings of unbelonging and bewilderment at being in the world intensified and manifested themselves in prolonged outbreaks of sobbing when I was alone in my bedroom. I could never explain what I was crying about but my grief was for some invisible missing part of myself. I didn't know what that part was but I was sure that if I had it I would have the same carefree outlook on life as my peers and would no longer feel that I was being rebuked for existing. I had no explanation then nor do I have one now for why I felt this way. There was no single, catastrophic event in my childhood that I could point to and say to myself: 'Ah, yes, it all goes back to that.' I sometimes felt as if my mind was like a recessive set of top teeth and my body a protruding set of bottom teeth and however hard I tried I couldn't align the two so that I could chew my way effortlessly through life.

When I began to experiment disastrously in my teens and twenties it was part of the same quest I had throughout my childhood to hear that satisfying click inside my head which meant that my body and soul were properly bolted together and could move through life as one. It was a long time before I heard it.

When I did play with other children, our games often descended into squabbles. Because I spent so much time alone or with adults, I didn't understand how to compromise and give way to the ideas of other children. So I learnt to block out the world and retreated increasingly into my own private, pain-free universe.

Unlike me, my mother was a highly sociable creature. She loved going to parties and when I was little she scooped me up in her arms and took me along with her, depositing me to sleep on a nest of coats in a bedroom. Often I slept through these nocturnal excursions, remembering only the sense of being lifted into my mother's unsteady arms and the fumes of cannabis, wine and sickly patchouli in the room. One night at a party, though, when I was four years old, I woke up disoriented in a strange room and started crying for my mother. I could hear music and laughter coming from the next room and stumbled sleepily towards it.

I tripped over lots of legs of people lying stoned and giggling on the floor.

'Where's my mummy? Where's my mummy?' I cried.

People smiled vacantly but made no attempt to help me. After a few minutes I found my mother sprawled on a sofa with a man I hadn't seen before.

She pulled me up on to her lap, giggled to her man friend and I drifted back off to sleep.

Some of the most joyful moments of my childhood were spent at my grandmother's house. My mother took me round there regularly and my world suddenly turned safe and cosy and warm.

My grandmother is a slim, energetic, well-groomed woman with a soft voice. She has always taken great pride in her hair. When I was a child, she laboriously washed, set and then dried it with a portable hairdryer. It looked like a plastic igloo placed on her head with a thick hose attached, which pumped hot air on to her curlers. Afterwards she doused herself with Elnett hairspray.

My grandfather had a reputation for being both distant and grumpy but he was always kind to me. I used to sit at his feet in the living room when I was three or four years old while he puffed away at his pipe and talked to me about how trains and planes worked and some of the wonders of nature.

Although my grandparents weren't wealthy, my favourite kinds of food – minced meat with carrots and mashed potatoes – were always in plentiful supply. I wished my mother would make me meals like that instead of the lentil atrocities she spooned into my mouth from an early age.

Apart from when she was doing her hair, my grandmother didn't seem particularly absorbed in herself. She always had time to teach me things: knitting, how to play 'Frère Jaques' on her old piano, the pleasures of shopping for food at the local shops.

'Can I stay with you for ever, Nan?' I used to say to her as I crept nearer and nearer to the heat and light of her dependable gas fire.

She shook her head and smiled but it looked as if she wasn't smiling inside.

'No, darling, I'm not your mum. You need to be with your mum.'

My grandmother offered to look after my brother after I was born when things began to go wrong between my mother and father. He became increasingly violent towards my mother and she thought it prudent to keep Tony away from him in case he started lashing out at him. It was supposed to be a temporary measure but by the time my mother had split up from my father Tony was so settled and comfortable with my grandparents that it was agreed he could stay there.

Sometimes my mother cooked comfort food for me like my grandmother made. 'Rhea, darling, come and have some fish fingers,' was a sentence I loved to hear.

Fish fingers symbolised the predictable, safe life my grandmother led that I craved to be a part of. I was never able to resist biting into the succulent rectangles of white fish with their crispy orange coating. Chewing on the processed cod made me feel safe and secure in a way that lentils never could.

2. WELSH CAKES, PUMPERNICKEL AND RUBBER FISH

At the age of seven my mother decided it was time for us to leave the urban decay of south London and head for the lush hills of Wales. I hated change and although I wasn't happy at school I didn't particularly want to leave and face the challenge of a different school filled with unfamiliar teachers and children.

My mother took me to a commune in the Welsh countryside. It was founded on the principles of self-sufficiency. Chickens marched across the yard and various kinds of food were grown in allotment-style patches of earth around the house. There were several other families living there and lots of children raced around the hillsides with the rather bemused sheep.

The commune's philosophy was for people who had spurned the capitalist rat race to live in harmony with each other and with nature. But rows were commonplace. People argued that the division of labour was unjust and that they ended up doing more to sustain the idyllic lifestyle than their fellow idealists.

Sometimes my mother and a group of friends from the commune would leave the big draughty stone house to go camping deeper in the countryside where they could bond even more closely with fields, trees and sky. They were all particularly fond of travelling up into the hills where nobody from society could disturb them as they celebrated nature's riches. Expertly dodging the sheep's carcasses and the crows hovering above them, my mother showed me the magic mushrooms she and the other adults picked and warned me to avoid the poisonous ones at all costs.

'Nature has many riches but not all are meant for us,' she said in a quiet and sombre voice. 'If we respect the earth and the things it yields we will be well provided for.'

I decided to look for some magic mushrooms. I thought maybe I would be able to do magic things if I ate them. I loved the idea of finding something magic growing in the ground on the windswept, emerald green hillsides, little creamy jewels dusted with earth. When my mother and her friends ate the mushrooms they became giggly and childish, a change of behaviour which I assumed must have been caused by the magical properties of the mushrooms. When my mother was in her tent I decided to eat some, hoping that something magic might happen to me as it had to Alice in *Alice in Wonderland*, when she swigged the potion marked 'drink me'. I swallowed a handful complete with the bits of earth which still clung to the stems. Magic things did indeed start to happen very quickly. The moors seemed to shrink and I became a powerful elf skipping from one grassy slope to another. I felt very safe and comfortable but at the same time very excited. I had no idea that at the age of seven I was having my first psychedelic trip.

My mother was twenty-nine when we arrived at the commune and almost immediately locked bodies and (she said) souls with Hans, a nineteen-year-old from Germany with long, golden curls. Hans was the boyfriend of my mother's whom I liked more than any of the others she had when I was a child. He was a kind and gentle young man who played with me and loved cooking.

After a couple of months the two of them decided that commune life was a bit too communal and we all moved into a rundown cottage in a remote Welsh village. The house had an old butler sink in the kitchen and several hundred daddy long-legs that raced across floors and up and down walls, oblivious of and indifferent to our arrival. I was terrified and screamed every time one of them startled me. The village's only nod towards the kind of civilisation I was used to in south London was two grocer-type shops which opened for three hours a day. Both had rather bare shelves with a few miserable pints of milk, loaves of bread and bags of earth-covered potatoes spread across the emptiness. They concealed the nakedness of the shelves as minimally as a fig leaf. A single bus a week transported villagers to the nearest town, which was ten miles away.

My mother enrolled me at the local school. The experience was excruciating. I didn't understand a word of the Welsh the other children chattered to each other in and they peered at me with my strange English accent as if I was no less alien than a Martian who had suddenly landed in their midst. My brother and grandmother visited us once. I was overjoyed to see them but they didn't stay long. My mother made a special kidney bean pie in their honour but my brother hated it and spat it back on to his plate. I was aware that he didn't like coming into this unfamiliar, disorganised world, which was so far away from the ordered life he led with my grandmother. Whenever my mother and I visited Tony and my grandmother I was overwhelmed with envy. My brother didn't know how lucky he was to climb into the same bed every night and sit at the same table every morning to eat his cornflakes. I thought that his obvious discomfort when he visited my world proved that he had the best deal while I had received the short straw. When we waved them off back to London I thought wistfully of the steaming plates of mince and mashed potatoes my grandmother served and the two cosy armchairs, their covering faded to a sludgy brown, which were placed on either side of the open fire in the living room.

However the expeditions my mother took me on did have some compensations. One of the joys of the 'Welsh period' was the gnome man. As an extension of my fascination with and fantasies about fairies and magic, I had developed an interest in gnomes. While fairies were unremittingly good there was a bit more ambivalence about gnomes, and trying to work out whether gnomes were a force for good or ill fascinated me. Through my mother I got to know an old man with a white beard who lived in the village. I was convinced that he was a gnome. He invited us round to his cottage, a small musty place crammed with junk of all kinds. I decided that he was a benign sort of gnome. He made pots of scalding tea and Welsh cakes for us and while he and my mother and Hans chatted about things I didn't understand he sat me down on his lumpy sofa and handed me a pile of books about gnomes. Sitting quietly with my mother somewhere I could see her and turning the pages of books with brightly coloured pictures of the endless variety of the gnome species, a delicious tranquillity washed over me.

Another pleasure was visiting a friend of my mother's who had a daughter the same age as me. The pair of us packed up thick, clumsy jam sandwiches and cycled off into the countryside. As soon as I was away from crowds of people I felt calmer, and the tightness in my chest eased. I loved seeing the moist green of the trees and grass blur as we cycled faster and faster down deserted country lanes. My mother took me to the beach and I learnt how to get the sand and water mix just right to build the most perfect, solid sandcastles. I always wanted to stay on the beach for ever. It was one of those places where I could seal myself into a small, safe world and feel nature running through my fingers and toes. The stag beetles scuffed the warm dust as I tried to chase them. The summers seemed hotter then than they do now, and longer.

My mother soon wanted to be on the move again. Portugal was our next resting place. I was almost eight when we boarded a ramshackle boneshaker of a bus called the Magic Bus. It provided a service which meandered through Europe and its clientele was almost exclusively hippies and other backpackers. It was the hottest, rustiest bus I had ever been on. I can still feel the red plastic of the seats welding itself to the backs of my legs as I munched on goat's cheese and slabs of cucumber. We camped close to a nudist beach that was far away from the main tourist areas. We stayed for a while, surviving off beach produce.

My life revolved around the beach. It was a free and happy time. The light in Portugal is very different from the light in England. The sky seemed higher and more turquoise and rays of sun bounced off the clear sea water all day long, making the waves look like liquid diamonds. Like all the other naked hippies, my skin turned a tough shade of brown. I wasn't conscious of everyone else's nakedness or my own after the first few days. It was nice not having to get dressed in the morning or undressed at night and my mother commented with pleasure about the lack of washing. We only put clothes on when we went into the nearest small town to stock up on bread, milk and other essentials. Fish became our staple diet. There were many picturesque rock pools where we dangled our nets in search of shrimps, crabs and limpets. I enjoyed the shrimps and the crabs but the limpets were a different genetic ballgame altogether. Munching on them was more difficult than trying to saw through a handful of rubber bands. When we were reduced to chewing limpets we knew that the money had well and truly run out and that it was time to leave.

Hans contacted his parents in Germany and they agreed that the three of us could move in with them for a while. I was eight years old and longed to settle down in one place. Hans continued to be kind to me. He talked to me about some of the German customs which he despised.

'If you cross the road when the traffic lights forbid you to do so this is unacceptable to most Germans. They will see it as their civic duty to mow you down for breaking the rules,' he joked. I didn't understand quite what he meant but years later when I thought back to my time in Germany I began to realise what he had been talking about.

Hans' parents lived in an immaculate shuttered house on the edge of a forest packed with fragrant, dense, bottle-green trees. The downstairs of their house appeared to be some kind of restaurant laid out with a handful of tables covered with red checked tablecloths. But eerily no diners ever seemed to cross the threshold. I was shocked when I watched my mother and Hans sunbathe naked in his parents' back garden one hot summer's day. We stayed with them for a few weeks but it seemed obvious to me that neither Hans' quiet, withdrawn father nor his dominating, precise mother took to my vague, dreamy mother and her child who stared at them but rarely spoke.

So my mother and Hans rented a tiny two-roomed house in the village. Our back garden opened out to the forest and I spent hours and hours, shaded by the cooling foliage, playing by myself, talking to myself and imagining myself to be a wood nymph invested with magic powers. Like the time spent with the gnome man, during the hours I played in the forest, free from the claustrophobic surroundings of our new house, I experienced a very pure form of happiness. The sense of being an outsider, which overwhelmed me yet again at my new German school, temporarily vanished.

As soon as I'd learnt how to communicate in German with my classmates, my mother decided it was time to move on again. We had been in Germany for less than a year. I never knew what prompted these decisions to abandon whatever precarious roots we had managed to put down in a new place. I watched my mother lovingly tend her spider and lemon balm plants and decided that the flimsy roots those plants put down were all she required to feel settled.

3. A COMMUNE AND A COMMON

When we arrived back in England my mother looked around for a new alternative community to join. We visited a large, airy house owned by the Hare Krishna community somewhere in the countryside. Although I found the members scary, living in a secure, solidly built house which we wouldn't have had to move on from every few weeks was enormously appealing to me. In the end, though, my mother decided it wouldn't be a good idea to throw in our lot so entirely with the organisation. I reasoned that as long as I could have my own bedroom and didn't have to get involved with shaving my head, wearing orange robes or lifting tambourines joyfully into the air, I'd be happy to move in. I was faintly disappointed when my mother, Hans and I trudged down the long gravel path back to the train station.

'Don't worry, love,' she said, absently smoothing my hair. 'I've heard of a really nice commune just outside Bath which has some space. We'll give that a try.'

My heart sank. I had hoped that we could find a proper house to live in. At last, a house like my grandmother's where traditional home cooking bubbled on the stove and

I could snuggle into the faded armchair by the fire. I couldn't hide my disappointment and pulled a face at the mention of the word commune.

'Don't look so down, darling. I've heard that this one is much better run than the one we stayed in in Wales.' The handfuls of solitude that I had carved into my daily life in Portugal and Germany became even dearer to me when I found out they were about to be snatched away. The thought of living in a noisy, crowded, hippy place filled with vague, smoky people and indigestible food made me feel as if my mother had inserted a lump of lead between my ribs that was dragging me towards the ground.

I was nine years old when we arrived at the new commune, a former Victorian psychiatric institution. With its tall grey-gabled windows and gloomy brickwork, it was the perfect setting for a Gothic horror story. I wondered if any of the former patients were hiding in the attics and I trembled.

As I had expected, the commune was full of noise and arguments and chaos. There were some old stables in the grounds where miscellaneous piles of junk had been deposited. I spent hours by myself rifling through the junk, pretending that it was treasure. A dark-haired girl called Josie, who was far bolder than me, crept into the stables one day with one of her hands clenched shut.

'Guess what I've stolen?' she whispered conspiratorially into my ear.

I tried to guess what object was small enough and exciting enough to be concealed in the palm of Josie's hand.

'A gold ring?' I offered lamely.

'No, try again,' said Josie scornfully.

I couldn't think of anything else it could possibly be.

With her brown eyes shining with excitement, Josie unfolded her fingers to reveal a slightly crumpled cigarette.

She fished a damp box of matches out of the back pocket of her jeans and finally managed to get the cigarette lit.

She took an almighty intake of breath and coughed so badly I thought she was going to collapse. It didn't put me off, though. I took the cigarette off her and held it inexpertly between my thumb and first finger. I too started to choke. The taste and smell were so foul I thought I was being poisoned.

At that moment one of the adults heard the coughing commotion and came into the stable. Horrified, he snatched the cigarette out of my hand and trampled it to bits on the floor.

'The two of you are far too young to be ruining your lungs with that stuff. Leave it alone and come back to the house now. It's almost dinner time.'

My first experience of smoking was horrible and thrilling. I felt that Josie had unlocked an appetite for the forbidden in me that I had no idea I had. I planned and plotted ways to steal another cigarette so that I could smoke again but before I had an opportunity we were driven out of the commune.

A group of noisy, threatening police officers arrived around 2 a.m. a few nights later and told us we were living on the premises illegally and had until morning to get out.

I was absolutely terrified. To be jolted out of sleep by such harsh, angry voices made me burst into tears. My mother tried to hush me but I wasn't able to fall asleep again when they'd left. I lay under the covers, my teeth chattering with fear, until it got light.

After that we stayed in a few squats. One contained an Alsatian dog whose owner let him defecate in all the rooms; another had missing floorboards and large holes in the roof. I was terrified of the Alsatian. You wouldn't think that a dog could be triumphalist but this one was. After every poo he deposited on the floor he looked at me serenely and intently before wandering off into another room.

During this period we visited the female protestors at Greenham Common. Although I understood almost nothing of what was happening there, I knew that the soldiers and police in their stern, dark uniforms and the nuclear weapons, whatever they might be, were the baddies while the women encamped there were the goodies. We arrived one baking hot June day in my mother's battered old car. I found the women almost more terrifying than the soldiers. There seemed to be a lot of shouting going on between different women, bobbing in and out of brightly coloured tents; some of them, my mother said, were called teepees.

'Nuclear weapons are very bad, darling,' she explained, pausing for dramatic effect. 'Evil governments like ours and the Americans want to drop poisonous nuclear bombs on people which choke them to death and destroy their towns and villages. Lots of peace-loving women are camping at Greenham Common where the weapons are stored to try and get the government to dump the weapons for ever.'

I was very upset by the noise of the women shouting. My mother looked perplexed as she and Hans wandered between the tents and benders – sturdy tree branches shaped into semi-circles and covered in plastic and other waterproof materials. I think she had expected gratitude from the indigenous population but instead was met with a torrent of abuse.

One woman with cropped, spiky hair, dyed purple, wearing dungaree shorts, which looked a bit like the lederhosen I'd seen some of the German schoolchildren wearing, stomped out of her tent and placed her hands grumpily on her hips.

She spoke with an abrasive Cockney accent that didn't seem to fit with my mother's account of Greenham women. I'd imagined that they'd be gentle, dreamy sprites, not quite of this world, with the same sort of magical powers as angels to bathe the world in a pale yellow light of goodness.

''Ere, darlin', you can't bring a man into the camp. Were you born yesterday or what? This is women only, W-I-M-M-I-N, got it, love? Yer fancy man needs to scarper or there'll be trouble. It's bad enough being harassed by all them guards and police without being pestered by a strange man nosing around our living quarters. You're a traitor to your gender bringing him along with you. You should be ashamed of yourself.' She sniffed, waving her finger at Hans so violently that I was sure the gesture broke the camp's non-violence rules, which were posted up on various trees and gates. Hans, a man who never wanted to offend, started taking apologetic steps backwards, banging his head on a thick tree branch in his haste to cancel out his offence. Unlike Hans, my mother seemed unperturbed by the ticking off and was in no hurry to leave. More shouting ensued as more women poked their heads out of their tents and saw an enemy in their midst.

'We don't mind men joining our protests outside the base but he mustn't come round here,' said a grey-haired woman with a gentler voice and a slow smile. 'There's a sit-down protest on the road outside just beginning – why don't you come and join us there?'

Hans nodded gratefully, glad to have been offered a dignified way out of being the wrong gender.

Crowds of women accompanied by a few men were sitting down in the road, singing songs I'd never heard before.

The older woman who had led us away from the tents towards the protest sat cross-legged, rocking back and forth, half whispering, half crooning to herself: 'The lorries must not pass, the lorries must not pass.'

Large groups of grim-faced police and soldiers tried to move us on. I was terrified and clamped both my arms and my chest to one of my mother's arms. She pretended to me that all was well but I sensed that she too was rather alarmed. I don't think she'd expected a jaunt into the Berkshire countryside to save the world to be so violent and so unpleasant. My mother had always told me it was dangerous to stray into the road but suddenly she was encouraging me to sit down on the warm, sticky tarmac and not to move even though a juggernaut of a lorry was heading towards us. All my instincts told me to run away and find a pavement sanctuary somewhere but I obediently sat down beside her. A few women screamed as police dragged them away and punched them.

When my mother had told me that we were going to Greenham, I'd expected some sort of day trip to the seaside. Finding not only an absence of sand, sea and buckets and spades but also that the main entertainment was sitting in the middle of a main road, witnessing police violence and being shouted at by strange-looking women, was deeply unsettling.

My mother took hold of my hands, tried to unwrap them from their vice-like grip on her arm and said, 'Let's go.' She nodded to Hans and the three of us started running up the road to where the car was parked. I turned back and saw that the lorries were retreating and the protestors were clapping and cheering.

My mother was subdued for the rest of the day. She pulled out our picnic of lentil salad and heavy rye bread and bananas that had blackened in the heat. We sat in the car, all feeling rather mournful. Hans and my mother chewed their way rhythmically through the food and said little. I felt too upset to eat and although I didn't like to be seen crying, a few tears escaped down my cheeks each time images came into my mind of women being drag-scraped along the ground by police officers, like rag dolls. All I wanted to do was to get back home as soon as possible. There it was easier for me to seal myself into my own tranquil bubble. We slept uncomfortably in the car and drove home the following morning. The subject was never discussed again and my mother didn't suggest a repeat excursion to rid the world of nuclear warheads.

Apart from travelling to protests, we did have an annual family holiday of sorts. It consisted of hitchhiking to Wales and meeting up with various long-haired kindred spirits of my mother. I would have much preferred the kind of package holiday to the Costa del Sol that girls at my school went on. They came back tanned and animated, jabbering about feasts of paella and scalding sun and amorous waiters who drove their older sisters crazy. Nobody but me hitchhiked to Wales for their holiday.

One year, when I was ten years old, we met up with my mother's friends on a pristine stretch of beach. The atmosphere was festive. The adults smoked cannabis, ate copious amounts of bean stew and tipped homemade wine carelessly down their throats. Snatches of conversation wafted past me on the evening breeze. 'Off to the music festival in Hamburg . . . Great dope there, saving to get to San Francisco, bit hard to hitchhike across the Atlantic though, ha ha . . .' I felt sleepy and tried to make a pile of driftwood comfortable enough to curl up against. But it was hard and damp and scratchy and I kept shifting restlessly from one shoulder blade to the other. Out of the corner of my eye I saw my mother stand up unsteadily. 'I'm going to make everyone a nice cup of tea,' she declared. A pot of water was boiling over an open fire. Everything happened so fast, I wasn't sure whether my mother knocked the pot of water over or someone else did, but suddenly my mother let out a blood-curdling scream. It cut through the vague, faraway atmosphere of the gathering like a gunshot.

My mother's feet were badly scalded. It was quite unbearable to look at the raw, blistered skin and over the next few days walking was impossible for her. It was distressing to see her in so much pain. Usually when I saw other people in pain the cause was something internal so

I could only approximate in my imagination how it felt. Looking at the mangled skin on my mother's feet, there was no doubt about the agony she must have been in.

After a few weeks of sitting on the beach with her feet propped up on a camping stool, my mother began to recover.

'You've been such a good girl, Rhea, I'm lucky to have you,' she said, leaning over and hugging me. 'There's a Hare Krishna festival on a few miles away. Would you like to go along? I'm sure there'll be lots of things for children to do there.'

Generally I loathed going to Hare Krishna festivals. To me the devotees had a scary otherworldliness about them. In fact, I wasn't entirely sure that they actually came from planet Earth. When they sashayed past, garish robes swaying and tambourines jangling, I tried to dig myself deeper and deeper inside the calm space in the middle of my head. One thing I adored, though, was the sweet, crumbly halva they handed out to everyone.

At this particular festival, I cupped my hands together when the halva was offered in the hope that they'd give me a double helping, then I ran off to sit behind a rock I'd discovered away from the noise. I lay back, closed my eyes and let little lumps of halva melt into sticky liquid in my mouth then trickle down my throat. I was truly happy.

Another feature of summer holidays was the de rigueur visit to Glastonbury. We went in the days before it became a huge commercial operation. I was mortified when my mother traded in our battered Citroën for a large bus that she painted green and purple with the Libran astrology sign on it. When she dropped me off at school in the Citroën I felt that I could almost pass for normal among my peers but when she acquired the bus and started delivering me in that, the humiliation was intense. I opted to walk to school after a couple of girls from my class spotted me getting out of it (I'd insisted my mother parked it round the corner from school) and giggled conspiratorially.

At Glastonbury I didn't feel quite so out of place rolling up in the green and purple bus. I remember watching Echo And The Bunnymen play one evening and looking up at the moon to see if it was doing all the things the band sang about. Glastonbury was a very safe place for children to run around and we were more or less left to our own devices. That suited us all fine.

To my delight my mother eventually decided to settle down in Bristol. She applied for and was given a Housing Association property. For a while I expected to wake up one morning and hear her announcing that we were moving on but as the months passed I realised that perhaps she was genuinely tired of never having a secure place to lay her head at night and secretly enjoyed a spot of routine.

I loved living in one place. I had a room of my own and felt that my clothes and books and Debbie Harry and Fun Boy Three records would be safe there and wouldn't vanish or be trashed by someone I didn't know by the time I got home from school. I continued to be a solitary child but I did make a few new friends, one a Hindu girl, Jasminder, who lived a couple of doors away. We used to walk along the back wall of our respective gardens, tightrope-style, to reach each other's houses.

She was an only child and even before we became friends we had sniffed out the information about both of us being alone and loners. I adored going to her house. Her grandmother plied me with sickly, sticky Indian sweets and the two of us watched wall-to-wall Bollywood movies. I couldn't speak Hindi but I soon managed to grasp what was going on with exaggerated plots and tales of unrequited love played out against a backcloth of singing and dancing and glittering, jewelled costumes.

Another friend I made was a girl called Rose who lived with her parents and brother in a huge house I called 'the mansion on the hill'. Both the children had their own bedrooms and their own playroom and they had an attentive mother who laid out plates of chocolate marsh-mallows and proposed picnics and other pleasures. I didn't particularly like Rose but each night I screwed my eyes shut and wished that I could wake up the next morning in Rose's bed leading Rose's life.

One of the things I liked most about our new settled existence was that my mother didn't always have a boyfriend attached to our lives. I had got along well with Hans but after we moved into the housing association property he and my mother began to drift apart. They squabbled over inconsequential things and eventually agreed to separate. I never saw him again. My mother had fewer boyfriends after that and none of them seemed to last as long as Hans nor did I like them as much. I loved being at home with my mother when it was just the two of us; when I felt that she had unlimited amounts of attention to lavish on me and when I didn't have to compete with a man.

4. THE REJECT GROUP

M y mother enrolled me at the local Rudolf Steiner school, beloved of hippy parents and rustic types who favoured organic, wholegrain food long before it became fashionable. I know that my mother was trying to do the best she could for me but I was uncomfortable with being on first-name terms with the teachers and the whole 'alternative' take on life and education. I kept on pleading silently: 'Give me normal, let me be like other children, don't force me to be different because you have chosen a different way to lead your life.'

All children are born with invisible instructions about the kind of childhood they will respond best to. I believe that this is something tattooed into the DNA and is resistant to an upbringing which attempts to lead in a different direction. My invisible instructions said 'conformity', being part of a group, identifying with others.

The school had some peculiar rules that I didn't understand. During an art class I drew a stark black and white sketch of a river scene in charcoal.

'No, no, no. We can't have black lines on our pictures,' said the art teacher, tutting. 'We're doing watercolours and your paintbrush must flow freely across the page without the coarse interruption of an inhibiting black line.'

I didn't understand what the teacher was talking about and I was cross because I felt my drawing was quite impressive. I sat quietly and said nothing but I felt very hurt. Some of the girls, dressed in tight T-shirts and ra-ra skirts, giggled behind their hands and looked admiringly at their own outline-free paintings.

I started analysing the behaviour of the popular girls who led different social groups within the school. Although I knew that I couldn't be one of them, I tried to replicate their skills within my own social group, which was branded 'the rejects' by the more popular pupils.

My reject group consisted of a girl with an unflattering pudding-basin hairstyle, square-framed NHS glasses, Argyll sweater and black nylon trousers that always seemed too short for her. Her mother was a teacher at the school, which didn't help her social chances. There were a couple of tomboys called Natalie and Rochelle who weren't girlie enough to fit in with the popular girls, a boy called Johnny who had scars across his body from the day his dressing gown caught fire and a boy called Bryan whom I particularly loathed – he brazenly excavated the contents of his nostrils and ate whatever he found. While I didn't particularly want him in my group of misfits, he did make up the numbers and I decided that on balance it was more important for me to be seen as having a large following than for all the members of my group to be socially acceptable.

The school was fond of staging productions of various classic plays and I was given a starring role as Titania in *A Midsummer Night's Dream*. Memories of magicking myself into a fairy as a little girl came back to me and as I flitted from one corner of the stage to the other, reciting strange, unrecognisable words, I felt that I had permanently left my own body and soul behind and transformed forever into this dreamy, mystical person from the past.

I led my reject group on fantasy excursions around the school premises. Taking my minions on archaeological digs was one of my favourite break-time activities. Using sticks and twigs we managed to dig up bits of charred pottery and various sweet papers. One day I managed to unearth broken pieces of china that together made up three-quarters of a milk jug. I was convinced I'd found a precious antique but Natalie brushed aside my grand idea.

'I bet one of the dinner ladies smashed it and chucked it in the bin and it rolled on to the soil,' she said pragmatically. Even though she was probably right, I felt wounded and annoyed that she had shattered my thesis.

At the age of twelve and a half my days of archaeological digs ended abruptly. My mother informed me that she was taking me on a youth hostelling holiday in Cornwall. I was furious. I wanted to go somewhere exciting on an aeroplane. I longed to lounge beside a swimming pool tiled in turquoise to make the water look extra inviting. I wanted to lick swirly ice creams into a neat round globe of vanilla on the cone and I wanted to practise my non-existent Spanish or French or Italian on a handsome, tanned teenager astride a Vespa. What I absolutely didn't want was to go youth hostelling in Cornwall. I could think only of my days in the scruffy communes in Wales and near Bath where we laid out our sleeping bags higgledy-piggledy on cold, hard floors. I had got used to having a room of my own and didn't want to forgo that luxury in the name of a so-called holiday.

In the end, though, I had no choice. Grumbling incessantly, I accompanied my mother. On the first evening of the holiday we had just bought some food and were crossing the road with it when I was swept off my feet. I had no idea what had happened to me and perhaps lost consciousness for a few seconds. I found myself lying in a heap in the middle of the road. I couldn't feel anything except an icy coldness, even though it was a warm, sticky night. My mother was screaming and I wondered what she was making such an enormous fuss about. It transpired that as I tried to cross, a car travelling too fast on the wrong side of the road hit me, lifted me up and over the bonnet and deposited me on the tarmac on the other side of the car.

My leg was badly broken, I had a head injury that caused bruising to my brain and my spleen was so badly damaged that it had to be removed. I spent three wretched weeks in Truro Hospital. I loathed having to be dependent on others for every movement and the most basic needs.

Eerily, although the accident came as a complete shock to me, I remembered as I lay on the table in Accident & Emergency that I had dreamed this moment two months ago. In my dream I was lying in a blindingly white room screaming, 'I can't move my legs, I can't move my legs!' As I lay there I cried out exactly the same words and felt the identical sense of desolation. My mother held my hand and wept a lot. Watching me shoot up over the car bonnet like a cannonball must have been extremely traumatic for her. Because I hadn't seen the accident happen to myself I couldn't appreciate the full dramatic impact of it.

'My poor, poor Rhea,' she said over and over again, stroking my matted hair. 'I can't believe this terrible thing has happened to you. I'm going to do everything to make you well again.'

While I couldn't absorb the impact of the accident from a bystander's point of view, I was all too aware of the extreme pain. As I lay in bed willing the painkillers not to wear off too quickly I started wondering if I'd been put on the earth by mistake. I couldn't see any purpose in my life.

One of my mother's curative strategies was to enlist the services of a Buddhist monk. She had previously taken me to various Buddhist retreats for quiet but doctrinaire days of chanting and insipid bowls of rice and vegetables so she had plenty of contacts in that world. Dressed in billowing saffron robes and with a shaven head, he sat by my bed chanting endlessly. I found the chanting both soothing and boring and after a few minutes of it I usually slipped into a deep, peaceful sleep. Whether it was the prayer or the impact of modern medicine, I did start to feel better. Feeling pain evaporate after living with it eating into your soul is a truly pleasurable feeling.

At last I was discharged from hospital, with a metal plate in my leg. I spent the next five months convalescing – and eating. I ate because I was extremely bored. A familiar cycle emerged of eating followed by self-loathing followed by more eating to try to drown out the self-loathing. I went to see the family doctor for a post-accident check-up. He didn't seem too interested in my general health but shook his head and said, 'You really should lose some weight, you know – you're too fat.'

I felt as if I'd been sprayed with bullets. For an adolescent of twelve and a half who felt even more dislocated from the world than usual because of my accident and enforced separation from my peers, no words could have damaged me more. While I can't entirely blame the doctor for the eating disorder I developed, I did feel that his harsh words acted as a trigger. I looked at the rolls of fat that pooled under my chin and across my stomach and thighs and worked out a plan.

It was a three-pronged strategy: starvation, laxatives from the health food shop and manic exercise. I allowed myself no more than 250 calories a day and bounded up and down in the living room for lengthy periods, dancing and doing extremely speedy sit-ups. To anyone who walked past the window I must have looked like one of those cartoon characters who perform everything at fast-forward speed. I experimented with making myself sick just for good measure but the mechanics of it defeated me. I managed to make my tonsils sore by poking my fingers around my throat but I failed to regurgitate any food and after a couple of days gave up trying. But even without the enforced vomiting the weight fell away. I had discovered an aptitude for dieting to the point of starvation. I didn't realise at the time that I was learning how to be anorexic.

Although my fat melted away, I still considered myself to be obese and ugly and took a lot of my anger out on my mother. I threw plates across the room, screaming, 'I hate you, you're the one who made me, how could you have made me so fat and ugly?' I had the sensation of a ballpoint pen pressing harder and harder into my flesh. When I was younger I'd had the same feeling, only then it was a mild pinprick. Over the years the pressure increased and increased like clouds sagging before a storm; after my accident everything exploded. My mother didn't know what to say when I raged against her. She realised that platitudes would be pointless and thankfully said nothing. She wanted me to be happy but didn't know how to help me attain that state of contented equilibrium which so often eludes adolescents. I wanted to have some control over my life and eventually came up with a plan. I demanded that my mother send me to a different school when I had recovered. She agreed, sensing that she was at the beginning of losing me and that I would slither away from any sensible arrangements she tried to make for me.

5. TRANSITION

U ntil the day I switched secondary schools, I was still recognisable as my free-spirited mother's daughter. The new school gave me the perfect excuse to cast aside the mohair sweaters of rainbow hues, the purple corduroy trousers and the squat Birkenstock sandals that my mother had proudly dressed me in for more than a decade. They were replaced first with ra-ra skirts and later pencil skirts with T-shirts and stilettos, a look one of my female friends referred to rather unkindly as the 'slutty house-wife' look.

Even though I now looked slimmer and cooler than I did before my accident, I didn't want to be at Rudolf Steiner any more where my fat geek baggage would be fresh in everyone's minds. A new school meant no history, no then-and-now comparisons and no awkward disentanglement from my previous social circle. Going to a tough comprehensive in inner-city Bristol was a joyful Year Zero for me. I was developing an appetite for extremes and wasn't happy with a mild personality makeover from misfit to unremarkably acceptable. I decided I was going to construct a totally opposite persona; I was going to become a hard girl. I felt bolstered by the fact that I already knew some of the pupils at the new school. I had talked to them in the local park where they and I hung around. I had started going into off-licences and, putting on a bizarre French accent, managed to persuade the shopkeepers to sell me cans of Thunderbird. I knew the park kids had seen me do this and were impressed. I felt that the illicit trips to buy alcohol were important building blocks in my new image. Once I'd started this fundamental image overhaul, I found that I couldn't stop. As soon as I made the decision to change myself, I went into an ultimately disastrous freefall. It was a very long time before I finally hit the bottom with a thud.

Mostly the components of the new me were easy to acquire. Attending almost no lessons was very important. The teachers rarely bothered to challenge those of us who bunked off daily. We held court in the girls' toilets, a smelly concrete block with clumps of wet toilet paper festering in pools of water on the floor. Me and my friend Carole didn't idle away the time, though. Both of us had discovered cannabis and smoked it with an almost evangelical commitment. Another girl at the school called Brenda had initiated me into the hazy delights of the drug. She had stolen it from her mother, who smoked it regularly. Brenda had bright rosy cheeks like the Topsy and Tim characters in children's storybooks. Her perpetually flushed cheeks gave a deceptive impression of innocence.

The cannabis made me giggle uncontrollably. Brenda's mother arrived home the first night we tried it, and, inured to the smell of cannabis, noticed nothing amiss.

'Would you like me to make you some pancakes with avocado, girls?' she asked.

'Yum yum, yes please,' we chorused, pretending to be wholesome characters from an Enid Blyton novel.

'These are absolutely divine,' said Brenda to her mother.

'Yes, absolutely divine,' I parroted.

'It's nice to see you're both in high spirits,' said Brenda's mother unsuspiciously.

Once initiated, I was keen to spread my passion for cannabis and Carole and I began dealing it in the toilets, a good spot to pitch our wares because this was a busy thoroughfare, particularly during the lunch hour. On a £20 bag of weed we were making a healthy £5 profit. I didn't know at the time that my business skills in this particular retail field would be finely honed in years to come. When Carole and I tired of dealing, we wandered out of the school gates and jumped on a bus to the St Paul's area of the city, which was known as the ghetto. We usually headed for the house of our favourite dealer Begsy and spent the rest of the day in a haze of smoke. Nothing felt real in the cannabis cocoon and both of us liked that. In Carole I had found a kindred spirit. She had been brought up in a children's home that she said had really messed up the inside of her head. She was a strikingly beautiful girl of mixed parentage and like me she hurled herself recklessly towards danger with no thought of the consequences. Both of us were like two-year-olds running blithely and repeatedly on to a busy dual carriageway. Around this time I started drinking vodka, as well as the Thunderbirds I was already used to, and experienced a different type of oblivion to the one I enjoyed with cannabis. I never had a moment of fear nor exercised any sort of caution when it came to ways of moving myself away from reality and towards some altered state or other. My mother did her best to control my excesses. She grounded me regularly but I outmanoeuvred her attempts at discipline. I became adept at clambering out of the bathroom window clutching a bottle of vodka. Later these climbing skills would help me survive a life-threatening situation.

I was attracted to smoking cannabis because I knew there was something forbidden about it. It also made me feel connected to being alive in a way that nothing else in my childhood ever had.

My mother had never been a bad parent to me but in her heyday she had dragged me across Europe with her love-and-peace-addled friends. We never remained in one place for very long. She was often absorbed with boyfriends and the combination of being in perpetual motion and getting accustomed to different men unsettled me. Embracing danger seemed to be one way of filling up a dark void that stretched like a gaping, bloodless wound from my heart to the pit of my stomach. I spent years shielding my eyes from the glare of that wound, always looking away, searching for some new excitement or other to blot it out. I only understood much later that turning to face it was the best way to make it disappear.

Cannabis was the prologue to my new life and Jerome was chapter one. We met in a musty corner shop, an Aladdin's cave of mingled spice smells, loaves of Sunblest piled next to boxes of Indian hair pomades with lavish Hindi inscriptions on them. After an extended session at Begsy's house, Carole and I were starving and gathered miscellaneous packs of crisps and biscuits into our arms. Jerome was in front of us in the queue. He was a black man, of Jamaican origin. I don't know why I was drawn to him but I completely and utterly was. He was short and very slightly podgy with a small goatee beard. He was wearing a loud orange puffa jacket that I instantly took exception to, but when he smiled his face became beautiful, lit by extra-white eye whites and perfect, dazzling teeth. He was bargaining for credit for a tin of sweetcorn with the shopkeeper.

'Oh, go on, Chai, you know I always pay you back. I'm coming into some money by 9 a.m. tomorrow morning and you'll be the first beneficiary. I've got my rice and corned beef cooking and it just won't taste the same without a fine sprinkling of sweetcorn.'

The way Jerome smiled, Chai couldn't help but smile back.

'All right then, Jerome, but make sure it is tomorrow morning. You'll bring my business to its knees one of these days.'

As he charmed Chai, Jerome kept turning round and grinning at us. I assumed that he was interested in Carole as boys and men fell at her feet with breathtaking predictability. But strangely, as he began bantering with us, he directed most of his remarks at me. I basked in the warmth of his attention.

'How you two lovely ladies doin' today?' he said, fixing his gaze on me. We looked rather obviously stoned as we swayed and giggled giddily. 'I'm Jerome. What's your names? That's a big pile of stuff you've got there. Looks like you girls got an attack of the munchies from puffing on that evil weed.'

Neither Carole nor I managed to mumble more than a couple of syllables so we carried on laughing. I found the fact that he'd got the measure of us so swiftly very appealing.

'Now that I've got my sweetcorn I can produce the perfect dinner but I haven't got anyone to share it with. Why don't you both come back to my flat and help me eat this food? I'm a brilliant cook.'

I could see that the usually daring Carole looked hesitant. Jerome was obviously quite a bit older than us – he turned out to be twenty-four – but I had no such reservations.

I craved an adventure and Jerome looked as if he might be the man to supply one.

I was just fourteen and a half and Carole was a couple of months older than me but we told Jerome we were both sixteen. He lived a couple of minutes away from Chai's corner shop in a bedsit. The floor of the communal hallway was thick with a well-trodden mulch of pizza takeaway and double-glazing flyers but Jerome's room was surprisingly tidy. I noted the pink nylon sheet on his single bed and cringed at the thought of my skin ever coming into contact with such a vile material. The corned beef and rice simmering on the stove made the whole flat smell sweet and salty. The three of us sat and ate. Jerome and I chatted but Carole said little. Conversation ran to the best cannabis dealers in St Paul's, the best blues clubs to hang out at and the nicest ways to while away seven or eight spare hours.

When we left, I said casually, 'I might pop in some time and say hi.'

He looked delighted.

'Yes, great, come over again soon. I'm often at home.'

I hugged myself with joy. The evening couldn't have gone better. Feeling captured inside a man's bubble of interest in me was intoxicating. Ex-fat, ex-reject me was the subject of a desirable older man's attentions. I'd never had a boyfriend before but I had a warm sensation that that was about to change.

'What a great guy,' I said to Carole as we walked home. 'How come you were so quiet, though?'

'That man is trouble, Rhea. Real trouble and I know. Be careful of him.'

Of course I ignored her warning and called round to see Jerome a couple of days later. To me he seemed very honest.

'You know I'd love to go out with you but I have got another girlfriend called Shirley. Trouble is I hardly ever see her cos she's always working.'

I told him I didn't mind about there being someone else and we started officially going out together although we rarely left his bedsit.

I didn't mind that either nor did I mind having sex with him, although I felt very little. Losing my virginity was something I felt relieved to get out of the way. The experience was disappointing given the stories we'd discussed at school about sex being something exhilarating and exciting. After a while Jerome began to get short-tempered. All I wanted was to sustain things in this new, adult world I'd walked into. I decided that I would do absolutely anything to keep him happy, calm and interested in me.

One day he told me sadly that he'd finished with his other girlfriend. He rarely mentioned her and although I spent an increasing amount of time at his bedsit she'd never appeared and I'd never met her. Looking back, I wonder if she existed at all.

In a masterful piece of manipulation, Jerome managed to make me feel sorry for him for the loss of his other woman, real or imagined.

'I couldn't handle it any longer, Rhea. One thing I didn't tell you is that she works as a prostitute. I couldn't bear thinking of her with all those dirty old men any more. Everyone had a piece of her and there was nothing left for me.'

I hugged and kissed him and stroked his hair.

'I can make you happy, Jerome, you know I can,' I whispered.

As the months went by, Jerome became more fractious when we were together. He started to criticise my inability to cook rice and my general uselessness around the place. His words lacerated my fragile self-esteem. Each stinging word chipped away at the veneer of hard, cool, thin Rhea to expose the old, fat, reject Rhea. I thought of Carole's warning but it was too late to heed it now.

'Why d'you never have any money, Rhea?' became one of his frequent jibes. 'I'm feeding two mouths here and all you contribute is a bit of weed now and again.'

As with his announcement about splitting up from his girlfriend, I didn't realise that he was laying an elaborate trap for me. From there it was only a short step to his suggested solution to the problem I was causing him.

A few evenings later, Jerome yelled at me about messing his rice up again.

'Just because you're a lousy cook doesn't mean I've got the money to keep on running out to buy more rice. Where d'you think the money is coming from?'

I hung my head. I thought I could bluster my way through playing a grown-up sixteen-year-old but it clearly wasn't working.

Then Jerome visibly softened. He sat down next to me on the nylon-sheeted bed and tenderly placed his arm around my shoulders.

'I'm sorry, Rhea, really I am. It's just that money is so tight. Shirley used to help out so money never used to be a problem.'

I wanted to help; I wanted to do anything I could to stop this new world I was clinging on to from ending. But I had no clue what I could offer to provide a salve for Jerome's agitation.

'I know a way,' he said suddenly, as if the idea had only popped into his head a split second before. 'It's a job you can do that wouldn't stop you from going to school. Out on the streets, y'know. A friend of mine can get you started.'

I knew what he was talking about. I knew very little about prostitution except that it involved women getting paid for having sex with men. I hadn't given any thought to the fear, the revulsion or the emotional damage the women in this line of work might feel. Because I wasn't interested in thinking about those things. All I wanted to do was keep Jerome happy and if he decided that this was the answer to our problems I would joyfully do it.

'Sounds good to me,' I said. He smiled a sleepy, lazy smile, put his finger over my lips to stop me saying anything more and kissed me lovingly for a long time.

A couple of nights later he told me I could get started. We'd barely discussed it since he proposed his new income generation scheme to me and he said little to me now as he led me to City Road in the heart of Bristol's red light area. I was only fourteen years old but had pretended to him that I was sixteen. I had often seen shivering women standing on various street corners. Without exception they looked thin and ill and prematurely withered. Cars crawled on with dipped headlights and the crumbling Georgian houses, painted in ice-cream pinks and pastel blues, looked more ghostly by night than in daylight. Although I had never spoken to any of those women I felt some kind of connection with them, a fascination with the hidden world they represented.

Jerome knocked on a door of a house in the middle of the red light area and a woman he introduced to me as Marla opened it. She looked unsurprised to see me and said little.

'See you later, Rhea,' said Jerome and sauntered off down the street, whistling softly. He had made as little fuss as if he was bidding me farewell at the door of Chai's corner shop. I had hoped for at least a little appreciation of what I was doing for him but none came.

Marla was friendly and at first glance attractive in a waif-like way although when I looked more closely at her she had the same ravaged look as the women standing outside. In the harsh light of the naked bulb hanging from the middle of her ceiling I could see every pock mark on her skin, the heavy, dead look in her huge brown eyes and the sickliness of her fuchsia lipstick. She was a white woman with light brown hair that frizzed dramatically around her tiny face. She poked a cigarette through a gap in the lipstick and lit it. I felt overpowered by the smoke and lit a cigarette myself, reasoning illogically that I might cough less if I smoked myself.

I felt uneasy but instead of thinking of what I was about to do I just kept thinking about Jerome and how pleased he'd be that at last I was bringing some money into our partnership.

She poured me a brandy and coke. I gulped it gratefully. The more warm oblivion the better.

Her large double bed was piled high with slightly grubby clothes, spangly tops and short skirts, along with lots of coats.

'We need to get you summat to wear,' she said in a husky northern voice. 'You're a bit bigger than me, though, so I'm not sure what'll fit you.' She found me a small beige jacket and a tight black knee-length skirt and banged a line of her lipstick on my unadorned mouth with very unsteady hands.

She stepped back and surveyed her work.

'You'll do,' she said, smiling. 'Don't tie yer hair up. Let it flow down long and loose – the punters like it like that.'

Marla worked on a street corner no more than six yards from her flat. She positioned me on the street corner opposite her regular spot. As she left me and crossed the road, the terror hit me. In a matter of minutes she had become a life support system for me. She knew how everything worked, she knew how to do the right thing, how to survive. As I stood alone on my corner, praying that none of the cars that slowed down to peer at me would stop, I briefly considered running away. But the thought of what Jerome would do to me froze me to the paving stone I stood on. I cringed at the thought of my fresh face, clear skin and shiny hair because it marked me out so clearly from the other women standing on the street. If I'd looked more sick and wasted I would have felt less exposed. But although I was more scared than I had ever been in my life, the street also held a fascination for me. It was as if there were two magnetic forces working within me at the same time – one repelling me and the other with equal force attracting me. That first night the latter force won.

A car pulled up alongside Marla. She leaned into it as the driver wound down the window. A couple of seconds later, she stood up straight and beckoned me over.

She jumped into the front of an old battered Volvo estate and told me to climb into the back.

'In yer get, sweetheart,' came a gruff voice from the driver's seat as I hesitated on the pavement. The car stank of old dogs, stale cigarettes and sweaty feet. I lit a cigarette to drown out the rotting smells with a fresher one. I felt removed from my body. It was someone else stepping into a stranger's car, sitting calmly in the back and inhaling deeply on a cigarette as if that's what I'd been doing all my life. This man, who hadn't yet turned round to let me see his face, was about to stop his car, peel off his trousers and have sex with me. What on earth was I doing here? How had I got myself into this? But swirling inside a fourteen-year-old's fear was the impulse that drove me to keep on finding a newer and better adventure than the last one. I told myself that if Marla and Jerome were supervising all of this, nothing could go too wrong.

The man parked his car under a bridge, slowly, deliberately killed the ignition and then turned to look at me. He was old and lined and bald and there was no trace of kindness in his face. He handed me £20 then climbed into the back seat and placed his hand firmly on my chest to move me from a sitting to a lying position. I pulled off my knickers and tucked them inside one of my boots. He had the biggest beer gut I had ever seen but was remarkably agile for a man of his size, wriggling deftly out of his trousers and underpants. Marla turned round, passed me a condom and then promptly turned to look away, staring steadfastly out of the car window.

I groped under his belly until I found his penis, put the condom on and waited for him to climb on top of me. I worried that he'd crush all the breath out of me and hoped he'd be quick.

As he heaved up and down, I kept my eyes fixed on the back of Marla's head. I decided that as long as I could see part of her, I'd survive this. He was mercifully quick and after emitting a long, contented grunt climbed off me, eased himself back into his clothes, calmly got into the driving seat and put his key into the ignition, obviously in a hurry for us to get out of the car.

'All right, love, that'll do for tonight,' said Marla when we got back. She smiled sadly at me as she slipped her key into her front door. My transition from the fat reject at the Rudolf Steiner school was complete.

6. THE LIFE OF GROWN-UPS

Jerome's indifference towards me grew. After my one-off experience of prostitution he hadn't mentioned it again. I held my breath and hoped he wouldn't. I was no longer spellbound by him and probably would have refused his request to go out on the streets again had he asked me.

We began to drift apart. The fact that I had proved I could earn money for him didn't seem to impress him. There was no formal farewell but we saw each other less and less. I knew that he had at least one other girlfriend but I no longer cared because I had met a new man who absorbed me absolutely.

I had turned fifteen and Leroy was thirteen years older than me. He was a tall, broad Jamaican man who worked for the council spreading tarmac on roads. He had a slow, wide smile that I adored. I often went to Bristol's blues clubs with some of my friends from school and I had seen Leroy there although we had never spoken. I was walking down the street one day when he drove past. He stopped the car and shouted out of the window: 'Oi, want a lift?' I jumped in, excited that maybe a new adventure was about to start. I was very impressed by Leroy's car. It was a typical ghetto car – a silver Ford Cortina with black grilles on the back window. We bonded over cannabis. Both of us sucked the drug into our lungs with equal passion and reverence while Bob Marley urged idealistic behaviour out of two gigantic speakers. On Sundays Marley was replaced with Ethiopian church music. Leroy shared a house in St Paul's with his brother, and I began to spend more and more time at their place, sleeping over at weekends and on an occasional night during the week.

There were plenty of young white women living with black men and I felt completely at home. Apart from the widespread smoking of cannabis, ghetto life was very conventional. Everyone was bringing up children and lots of the women had traditional 'three Cs' roles: cooking, cleaning and childcare.

I didn't see it that way at the time but I know now that I caused my mother inordinate amounts of grief when I was still living at home and had gone into wild-child mode.

'Make sure you're home by eleven,' she urged point-lessly.

I returned wearily at dawn, ignoring her worn, frantic expression.

'Please think about getting some sort of a job to support yourself if you're giving up on school. How about doing a college course which will give you a few skills?'

I shook my head and spent my days in a cannabis haze. I knew best. My mother's own cannabis consumption had waned by this time.

'Could you clear up your room so that I can at least get into it?' she pleaded reasonably.

I continued to pile dirty clothes on top of clean ones and to stub out spliffs on my bedside table.

While my mother sighed and wrung her hands about her brazen, wayward daughter, I felt that at last I was inhabiting my rightful skin. Rebellion seemed like a place where I belonged. For now I had given up on my earlier ambition to conform. It didn't seem as if it would ever happen and I was discovering that not conforming was a club in its own right where I felt very comfortable. At first I had felt at home rebelling against the strictures of school when I started playing truant and selling cannabis in the toilets and now I felt at home getting involved in an adult relationship. There were to be many more ultimately false feelings of belonging to come.

I looked forward to the day when I could move out so that my mother could no longer nag me. I simply couldn't wait to join the world of grown-ups.

What I didn't realise then was that I had choices, although some would take more effort and application than others. My understanding of the way life worked was that you stood in the middle of the motorway of existence and waited to see what hit you. I had spent all my life yearning for control over my destiny but it wasn't until much later that I understood that control must be worked for and doesn't fall into your lap. I assumed that the people whose lives I envied were simply luckier than me and that God had decided not to share any of humanity's good fortune with me. It was more than a decade later – having realised that this was a particularly paralysing form of self-pity peppered with self-loathing – that my life began to change.

At first I quite liked playing house. I was still nominally living at home with my mother but spent most of my time at Leroy's. Scouring the sink and hand washing Leroy's work overalls in the bath felt very grown up. My early attempts at West Indian cooking were atrocious but Leroy's brother taught me how to skin a chicken, season it properly and cook it to perfection with rice.

After a while the thrill of revolt against my mother paled. Sitting around smoking cannabis all day waiting for Leroy to finish rolling pungent asphalt on to bald roads became tedious. I was still very preoccupied with food and while I allowed myself to eat sparingly I remained terrified of ever getting fat again. I rationed myself to a piece of toast and a cup of tea in the morning and a bowl of soup in the evening with hardly anything in between, and that way I managed to hover just under a size eight. Still I wasn't satisfied with my size and longed to be slimmer.

Leroy was scornful: 'You white women, always dieting. We men like something to get hold of in a woman,' he used to say as he tucked into the huge plates of chicken and rice which I cooked for him but only picked at myself.

Obsessing about my weight and keeping house for Leroy were becoming dull. I decided that at the ripe old age of sixteen it was time to move on to the next stage of my life. Leroy and I agreed to stop using contraception and giggled about making babies. Within months one had duly been made, or the beginnings of one, at any rate. I was delighted. I was excited to be embarking on yet another adventure.

I broke the news excitedly to Leroy but he reacted coolly.

'How many weeks gone are ya? You need to get down to da doctor's, girl.' He gave me a three-quarters smile, one which didn't break out fully across his cheeks.

He didn't offer to accompany me to any of my scans or antenatal appointments and instead my mother came with me. She had warned me before I started a relationship with Leroy that she would be furious if I got pregnant and so when I broke the news to her she was unsurprised and said little.

I felt horribly sick for the first five months. As soon as I'd been sick I wanted to eat and as soon as I ate I'd be sick again. It was a tiring cycle. I continued to keep house for Leroy and his brother, to scrub his overalls and to present him with a cooked meal when he arrived home from work. I hardly gave a thought to the implications of being pregnant or what childbirth would be like. And I certainly didn't think about the responsibilities of bringing up a baby. It was as if I was only able to inhabit the very immediate present tense. I didn't want to think about the past and was incapable of envisaging the future. I was given a council flat and Leroy moved out of his home into mine.

The first time I gave any real thought to the process of having a baby was when I woke up with sharp, rhythmic pains in my stomach at 5 a.m. nine days before the baby was due.

'I think I'm in labour,' I said, nudging Leroy out of a very heavy slumber.

'You can't be – it's not due for another nine days. Just go back to sleep.' He turned over and pulled the covers tightly around his head.

I wasn't convinced that there were nine days to go and, panicking that the baby might plop on to the bedroom floor while Leroy was still sleeping, I threw on a dressing gown, slipped on a pair of shoes, and waddled to the phone box down the road as there was no phone in the house.

'I think I'm in labour,' I said breathlessly when I was put through to the maternity unit.

The midwife sounded calm and even on the other end of the phone.

'How far apart are your contractions, darling?'

'About every six minutes,' I yelped as another one rolled through me.

'Best come in as soon as you can. Have you got someone who can bring you or do you need an ambulance?'

'Oh, my boyfriend will bring me in – he's got a car,' I said proudly.

But when I got home and told Leroy that I was officially in labour and needed to get to hospital, he shrugged through his sleep and said he'd drop me off at my mother's house on his way to work.

'Childbirth is women's stuff. I'll come and see you when all the blood and goo has been cleaned up.'

I was devastated that Leroy didn't want to be there for his baby's entrance into the world. We'd never discussed the birth and it had never occurred to me that he'd choose not to be around.

By the time he dropped me at my mother's I was practically crawling on all fours. Leroy said he'd see me later and went off to roll tar. In the sea of pain, I realised at last that he cared nothing for me. It didn't help finally knowing that.

My mother called a taxi and tried to soothe me on the way to the hospital.

'Soon you'll have a lovely little baby and you won't even remember the pain,' she said.

'I don't want a baby, I don't want to be pregnant, I just want this pain to stop,' I told her.

Once I was installed in the labour ward, I became demented with pain. I gripped my mother's hand so tightly I drew blood.

Finally Paul arrived. His hands were outstretched as if to say hello to me and invite an embrace. His skin was almost as white as mine and although I had been entirely faithful to Leroy, I worried that he would accuse me of giving birth to another man's child. When Paul was placed on my chest I went into shock. I looked down at his scrunched-up face, the black splash of hair on his tiny head and his diminutive fingernails, which looked as if they'd been sketched but not yet coloured in. I couldn't believe that he was mine and that making sure he ate, slept and lived from now on was entirely down to me.

My mother was very pleased to see him. Her reservations about the pregnancy faded as she cradled him in her arms.

'He's an absolute beauty. He'll have all the girls running after him in no time at all,' she giggled. She called Leroy to tell him the news but judging from her subdued expression he hadn't downed his asphalting machine and jumped three feet into the air at the news that he had a son.

'Leroy says he'll be along to see you after work,' she said quietly.

I had had visions of him tearing through the swing doors of the hospital and wrapping Paul and me in an enormous hug. I thought that providing him with a child would make things better between us but his indifference at the arrival of the baby was the way things were going to be from now on.

He arrived at the hospital at 7 p.m., with a crumpled brown paper bag of tangerines. I took it disappointedly. I'd been hoping for an ostentatious bunch of flowers like all the other new mothers had, jostling the orange squash and plastic cups out of the way on top of their lockers. Leroy held out his little finger for Paul to wrap his hand around but he didn't pick him up. I cried all night long, my quiet sobs unheard above the intermittent wails of all the newborns. 'What have I done? What have I done?' I said over and over again to myself. 'I'm sixteen, I'm with a man who doesn't love me and I've got this tiny scrap of a screaming thing entirely dependent on me.' I knew at that moment that my mother had been right but it was impossible to rewind the last nine months of my life. Somehow I had to survive and to make sure that Paul survived.

I hadn't put much weight on when I was pregnant but was appalled that I couldn't zip up my jeans once I returned home. I hadn't been quite so obsessive about keeping my weight down because I didn't want to do anything to harm the baby. My stomach had sprung back to its pre-pregnancy flatness but somehow my organs had rearranged themselves so that my body took up more space than it did before I got pregnant. I vowed to go back to my toast and soup regime.

Having Paul changed things at home. Leroy expected me to keep house even more meticulously than I had tried to do before so the drudgery increased. Paul and I became extremely close. He was in my arms day and night and everywhere I went he was with me. My early despair about him in the hospital vanished. My mother came round regularly to help me with the baby but Leroy did nothing. I had seen so many scenes of contented family life on TV and thought that once Leroy and I had a baby the three of us would morph into this wondrous structure. But it never happened. I got better and better at looking after Paul all by myself. He was more than my flesh and blood; he became almost a part of my body. Whenever I put him down during the day I felt as if I had lost a limb. Leroy developed no such attachment to his son. He came home every evening, not only expecting his overalls to be washed, dried and folded and his meal to be on the table but also that the house would be immaculate. He ran his fingers along the tops of doors to make sure that they were dust-free.

'I expect my girl to keep the place nice,' he said, when I looked at him questioningly. I tried to protest and told him that I'd been scrubbing and polishing all day long but I was unable to defend myself against him.

'I've cleaned the cooker Leroy and I've scrubbed the floors, can't you see how they shine?' I pleaded.

'Ah yes, but you've not bothered to empty the washing machine or clean the bathroom. What have you been doing all day, you lazy bitch?'

It was too wearing to argue any more with him. By the time he got home from work I was invariably exhausted because of a lack of sleep and the sheer physical hard work of maintaining some semblance of order in the flat. I slumped on to the sofa and shrugged. It was very important for him to win all the arguments and I didn't have the strength to do anything but surrender. Part of me still wanted to please Leroy and I felt that if I argued too fiercely with him it would turn him against me.

I was becoming increasingly disenchanted with my life. And Leroy seemed increasingly disenchanted with me. However much I cooked and polished and folded, it wasn't good enough for Leroy. I became more and more subdued, trying desperately not to rouse him to anger. I was terrified that his escalating resentment against me would eventually progress to physical violence. On a few occasions he had raised his hand to me as if he was about to strike me and once he'd lifted a heavy glass ashtray and made as if to throw it at me. Although he had never actually struck me I felt it was only a matter of time and when he came home from work in a bad mood I trembled.

I had joined a group for young mothers and babies. They were all single and when I talked to them about my restrictive home life they encouraged me to leave with Paul and strike out on my own.

'Look, Rhea, you really don't need a man in this day and age,' said my friend Pauline, who had a little girl called Grace and had not been in touch with the father since she had conceived. 'It's better to be by yourself than to be with someone who constantly holds you back. I want to bring my little girl up with my values, not the values of someone I don't respect. You don't want Paul's first memories of his father to be "Have you washed my overalls yet?"' I thought carefully about her words and knew that she was right. But cowardice prevented me from leaving. I was not only scared of what Leroy might do if I walked out on him, I was also concerned about how foolish I would look to friends and family, particularly my mother. Leaving Leroy would be admitting that the whole expedition into premature adulthood had been a terrible mistake.

I adored Paul and felt increasingly that as long as he and I were together everything would be OK. Having a little person who loved me, needed me and was never going to leave my side filled me with a kind of happiness I hadn't experienced before. He had a trusting grin and never failed to laugh infectiously when I blew raspberries on his stomach or made 'yum yum' noises in his ear. Just as I knew every crease of his silken-skinned fingers and toes, I also knew all his different moods, what would startle him, delight him and what would make him cry. Paul became my world.

Friends started whispering that Leroy was being unfaithful and that I should hold my head up high and walk out. Before I could do that, the violence I'd been holding my breath against exploded with the dazzling suddenness of a firework.

Leroy and I were sitting in his car when he accused me falsely and pointlessly of infecting him with genital herpes. It turned out that a woman he had been unfaithful with was the culprit – I had been entirely faithful to him. He had imprinted on me too deeply the demand for loyalty for me to deviate from his expectations. Straying had never entered my head, much less been an option.

'You fucking whore, you've contaminated me with your sleeping around. I'll never be able to get rid of this herpes thing now I've got it. What the hell have you done to me? No woman of mine goes around being unfaithful and picking up diseases without getting punished for it.'

I was so stunned that no words of self-defence came out of my mouth. 'I . . . I . . .' was as far as I got.

Before Leroy raised his hand to me I knew he was going to do something terrible. I had never seen him so engorged with rage. He looked like a black pudding stuffed so full the skin was about to split. As I cowered all I could think of was how insane I had been to want to rush into adult life with him. I longed to be back inside my imperfect childhood.

He picked up an empty beer bottle and started hitting me about the head and body with it. It was very thick glass and miraculously it didn't break. The car was parked outside a busy nightclub on a main road and lots of passers-by saw him stinging me with blows to the chest and the abdomen. I feebly tried to cover myself with my hands. Out of the corner of my eye I could see them peering into the car, dispassionately assessing the situation and then continuing on their way without making an attempt to intervene and save me. It made me feel as if Leroy and I were the only two people left on the earth and that we were providing the people of a separate planet with entertainment through a car-shaped TV screen. When the blows stopped raining down, I shivered with loneliness. I ran out of the car weeping but had nowhere to go except back to the flat I shared with Leroy and his brother.

The shock of the assault left me reeling for days afterwards. I was so bruised I found it difficult to walk. No one had ever struck me before and I knew with the certainty that comes from fierce injuries that I had to run before things got worse. Leroy had an ex-partner whom he had a daughter with. The following day he confessed to me that he had been sleeping with her as well as with me.

'Turns out it was her not you who gave me the herpes, I got the slag to admit that she was sleeping around,' said Leroy. And that was as far as the apology went. I knew that I had to leave but that Leroy wouldn't let his 'property' go freely.

So I hatched an elaborate escape plan. A couple of friends who had a pet monkey offered to drive me away from Bristol, where we were living, to London, where my brother lived. The appointed time was the following Saturday afternoon when Leroy was shopping for new electronic equipment for his music centre with his brother. I knew that he would be out for hours, poring tediously over each gadget before deciding which one to buy. I dived into the car, hiding on the floor in case Leroy spotted me. The journey felt like some kind of hallucinogenic experience. As I crouched on the slightly damp floor of the battered old Fiat and Paul slumbered unaware in his car seat, the monkey leapt from one side of the back seat to the other. My friends Jan and Pam sat in the front, seemingly unaware of the back-seat action.

Pam drove at more than 90 miles an hour and every so often called out cheerfully, 'Only another fifty-five miles to safety,' 'Only another thirty miles to safety.' Miraculously all the humans in the car and the monkey arrived without broken bones or life-threatening injuries. At last I was safe from Leroy but not, alas, from myself.

Some sixteen-year-olds who give birth turn out to be excellent mothers. Contrary to the feckless stereotype, many want to keep house and have a tiny creature to love and nurture and offer stability to. While I loved Paul more than I'd ever loved anyone in my life, I simply wasn't ready to spend my days and nights polishing the floor and playing gooey baby games. Escaping from Leroy made me feel free but instead of counting my blessings and pulling back from the high-risk choices I was making, I launched myself with even greater force than I had in Bristol on to London's pub and club scene. I had stayed with my brother for a few weeks and then found a small flat to rent. I cultivated babysitters, often teenage girls, who lived in flats close to mine, so that I always had a plentiful supply to choose from when I wanted to go out.

I didn't want responsibility, I wanted oblivion, and I felt I deserved it after everything I'd been through with Leroy. I didn't understand that I was too immature to face and embrace difficult emotions. One of the very few things I remembered from school was a line from T. S. Eliot: 'Human kind cannot bear very much reality.' I had no understanding of how to process painful emotions, to absorb the shock of them and to neutralise them so that they didn't damage or destroy me. All I wanted was to experience pleasure and joy. I didn't know any way to find these feelings by connecting with other human beings so I turned to chemicals to manufacture the human emotions I craved. With Paul in the care of a string of babysitters, I partied with ecstasy and speed. Speed did what it promised to do. Everything became fuzzily faster. Ecstasy was peculiar. The first time I tried it I didn't particularly like the effects but there was something about the drug which made me keep on taking it. It became unthinkable to go to a club with the dance music beating insistently into my brain without taking an ecstasy pill.

I was very apprehensive when I decided to experiment with it. I'd heard that it was best to take half a pill at first in case it gave you a funny turn. I was in a dark, dingy basement of a squatted warehouse. The party had been organised by a group called Spiral Tribe. They issued a phone number to those in the know and then we had to keep on calling different numbers all day until the venue was revealed at the last moment. This secretive build-up to the party made the whole thing much more exciting. I was with a few friends and the seven- or eight-hour prelude to finding out where the venue was made the experience even more thrilling. The drug I bought was a red and black capsule called Dennis The Menace and it couldn't be broken in half so I swallowed the whole thing. For the first half an hour I felt nothing. Then suddenly my legs started to crumble under me. I was standing at the top of a moth-eaten flight of stairs. It was physically imposs- ible for me to walk down the stairs to the chill-out room in the basement so I sank into a heap and bumped down the stairs on my bottom. In the chill-out room were lots of other people, mainly white hippies with thick, rope-like dreadlocks, who also couldn't walk. We sat in a pile talking gibberish and thinking that temporary paralysis of the legs and the insides of our minds feeling like clothes on a washing machine spin cycle were extremely cool. Deeper than the desire to be fashionable and to belong was a sense of panic. I didn't like feeling so out of control. But after a few hours the effects wore off.

I persevered and within a few months I could neck six or seven pills in a night and feel secure enough on my feet to dance for hours to dance music that I never would have listened to stone-cold sober. I had a few brief and meaningless relationships during that period. I fell into the arms of anyone who I thought could make me feel better about myself. But invariably the initial interest they showed in me swiftly turned to a desire to control me. Sensibly I walked away. But at the end of a blurred night in the pub this instinct to protect myself deserted me. I brought home a man called Billy. He seemed vulnerable and needy and he caught me off my guard. Of all the disastrous decisions I made in my life, allowing Billy over the threshold was probably the worst.

7. BILLY

Billy said he was living in a grotty hostel and asked if he could stay over for a couple of days. I had no idea that he had escaped from prison and was on the run. I never got to find out what crime he had been convicted of. His sad little-boy-lost act won me over and I let him into my flat and my bed. For a few weeks he was gentle and attentive. Leroy and Jerome had been gregarious and charismatic. I decided that maybe I was better off choosing a quieter, more self-effacing man. Soon I knew that I wasn't.

The honeymoon period was horribly short. I had run down to the shops to buy a pint of milk one day and left Paul, who was now three, with Billy four weeks after he moved in. I returned and to my horror he was dangling Paul upside down by one leg. Paul couldn't stop screaming. I immediately grabbed him.

'What on earth are you doing to my son?' I yelled.

He grinned sheepishly. 'Just a little experiment about gravity. No harm intended.'

But he did intend harm. Cruelty was marbled through every cell of Billy's body, and after the dangling incident he didn't bother to conceal it any longer. He made Jerome and Leroy look like adverts for the very best the male species could offer. He was preoccupied with multiplying the ways he could be malevolent and spent a great deal of time planning his attacks on me and Paul. Billy understood that the threat of doing something could terrorise even more than actually doing it. He smoked enormous amounts of crack, which heightened his natural paranoia.

He perpetually accused me of cheating on him.

'You fucking whore, I'll get you back for this. Don't think you can be unfaithful to me and get away with it,' was one of his favourite lines.

'What do you mean, Billy?' I asked, quaking. 'You hardly let me leave the house. It would be physically impossible for me to conduct an affair with anyone. You know you're the only one for me.' I knew my words sounded hollow but placating him at all costs was vital to my survival.

When he first moved in, I carried on going to the pub where I had met him, getting babysitters to stay with Paul, taking speed and, if I went clubbing, ecstasy. By day I shopped and cooked and cleaned the flat. We lived on benefits that didn't stretch very far. It wasn't long before Billy put a stop to me going to the pub.

'I don't want no woman of mine frequenting those establishments. From now on you'll stay at home and you'll do as you are told.'

I knew few people in London and the nature of pub life was that people drifted in and out the whole time. When I stopped appearing, I wasn't missed. Then Billy started clamping down on my daytime movements, again accusing me of having an affair.

'You're not to be trusted, slag. I've got no alternative but to lock you in. I'll do the food shopping from now on and I'll do the cooking too. The food you cook is so disgusting I think you're trying to poison me.'

He couldn't stand Paul and whenever he cried, Billy yelled, 'Shut that fucking brat up or you'll pay, you bitch.'

Paul was terrified of the shouting. I rarely raised my voice to him and he wasn't used to any kind of violence. I spent all my time when Billy was in the house cuddling him and turning his head towards my chest to muffle any sound if he started to cry. Billy had started to beat me and I desperately hoped that he wouldn't turn on Paul.

'Please God,' I prayed, although I wasn't a believer. 'Let him take his rage out on me but not on Paul.' I wasn't using any drugs at all once Billy started locking me up. Firstly because I no longer had no access to them and secondly because I felt I couldn't afford to let my mind either dull or race chemically. I had to be stone-cold sober just to survive.

He started harming Paul – he burnt his feet with a cigarette and twisted his little arm so hard it broke. The screams of agony were unbearable and I heard the bone snap. Billy accompanied me to casualty and watched over me while I lied that Paul had fallen off the sofa when my back was turned for a moment. Living with Billy I genuinely believed that I could die at any moment. I was too frozen with fear to mount any kind of challenge against him. I kept thinking that if he killed me something terrible would happen to Paul. Although I couldn't protect Paul from Billy's attacks, things would be so much worse if I wasn't around.

Billy loved knives. He liked nothing better when he returned home from the pub than to switch off all the lights, blindfold himself and play the knife game. This involved throwing his knife up into the air. Paul and I had to guess where the knife, which he named Betsy, was going to fall and duck before it gouged out one of our eyes or embedded itself in our scalps. The terror we both felt was unspeakable. When he played this game I was more convinced than ever that one or both of us was going to die. On one of the rare occasions when he allowed me to go out with him, he took me to meet a group of Triads in Soho.

Triads are ruthless Chinese gangs who are concentrated in the Soho area.

'If you put a foot wrong, Rhea, these nice gentlemen will go round to your mother's house and then to your brother's house and do a good job on them, understand what I mean?' One of the Triads nodded gravely at Billy's threat. Then Billy marched Paul and me back to the flat and locked us in. I could see no way out.

Billy slept with Betsy the knife under his pillow. One night, as he snored beside me, I decided that the only way Paul and I were ever going to escape from him was if I stabbed him. Impulsively I slid my hand as furtively as I could under his pillow. I felt the coldness of the knife and inched it towards me as gently as if it was a spider's web that could disintegrate at any moment. I eased it into my hand. Billy was breathing evenly, his broad body making a wall in the bed. I knelt next to him and held the knife up, ready to plunge it down into the centre of his chest the way I'd seen it done in films. At that moment Billy jumped up and started snarling. He hadn't been asleep at all and was waiting for the optimum moment to pounce. He punched me hard in the face.

'Don't bother trying any funny business with me, bitch. Don't forget I'm a whole lot smarter than you are.'

I feared more blows but he slumped back on to his pillow and, holding the knife firmly in his left hand, went back to sleep, or at least appeared to.

Maintaining the same level of viciousness wasn't satisfying for Billy. Intensifying his variegated assaults on us appeared to be an addiction even more compelling than the crack he smoked.

I didn't own a mobile phone but Billy did and one day he carelessly left it lying on the sofa when he went to the pub. Not knowing how much time I had – sometimes he returned very quickly from the pub – I dialed my mother's number.

'Mum, it's me, Rhea.'

'Are you all right? You sound dreadful. Has something happened?'

'I can't talk for more than a minute. I'm renting a flat in Balham. Why don't you come down to stay. I'm sure Paul would love to see you.'

I gave her the address and she told me she had a few days free the following week and would come down then. I was overjoyed. I didn't know how she could help me escape but at least now I had a chance.

I didn't tell Billy that she was coming until the doorbell rang. He had a habit of shouting brusquely through the door before opening it: 'Who is it?'

'It's Rhea's mum come to visit,' she shouted through the closed door. Her voice sounded soft and tinkling next to his. Never in my life had I been so glad to hear it.

For the duration of her visit Billy transformed. Doors were unlocked and edible meals were cooked. But an hour or so after my mother arrived Billy grabbed me when I walked into the bedroom to fetch a cardigan for my mother who felt chilly.

'Don't try any funny business like escaping, bitch. I know where your mum lives and I'll go after her. I can tell you now it won't be a pretty sight.'

Despite Billy's pathetic attempts at being human I could see that my mother was very worried. As soon as she got home she contacted Social Services and two female social workers did pay a visit. This angered Billy more than anything had ever angered him before. When the doorbell rang he did his usual trick of asking who was there.

When a strong female voice called out, 'Social services, can you open the door please?' his face became thunderous. He grabbed Paul and his knife and hid in the cupboard with him. 'Tell that interfering busybody that Paul is at a friend's house and everything here is absolutely fine. If you don't Paul will get it in the neck and I really, really mean that.'

I opened the door and tried to impose a normal smile on my mouth.

'Oh, hello, Miss Coombs, my name is Maria, I'm a social worker with Lambeth Council and I'm here responding to a complaint we've received from your mother about your circumstances.'

'Oh, really?' I said, trying to look puzzled. 'I think she's just trying to cause trouble. Paul is round at my friend's house at the moment but as you can see everything's absolutely fine here, there aren't any problems. Come in and look around for yourself.'

The social worker peered into the flat, could see nothing immediately amiss and declined my offer to come in.

'Well, everything looks all right,' she said doubtfully. My performance obviously wasn't entirely convincing. 'Here's my card. Call me if you need anything or if any problems arise.'

'Thank you,' I said, trying to smile again but not managing it. I closed the door and allowed tears to roll down my face. I had closed off my only escape route. I was sure that the conditions of our captivity would be strengthened from now on.

Billy emerged from the cupboard holding Paul, who had started to scream. I assumed that he had slammed his hand over Paul's mouth to keep him quiet while the social worker was at the door.

'This calls for a serious punishment,' said Billy. He began to smile.

He grabbed Paul and shoved him forcefully on to a chair. Then he rummaged in the kitchen drawer for some string and bound Paul by the chest to the chair. 'You're going to stay awake all night now, boy,' he said. Paul sat bolt upright for the first hour but then the sheer monotony of the position made his head loll forward and his eyelids droop. Every time his eyes closed Billy punched him in the face. He screamed and sat upright again but soon the cycle started to repeat. I sat on the sofa and watched, more tortured than I thought it was possible to feel. Questions danced around my mind in a frenzy.

Should I try to grab Billy from behind and wrestle him to the ground? I knew it would be futile. Paul and I had both become very skinny because Billy either didn't allow us to eat or cooked inedible food. He was much stronger than me and I knew it was ultimately pointless trying.

'Punch me, Billy, tie me up, but please, I beg you, leave that innocent little child alone,' I screamed.

'No, bitch, you'll suffer much more this way.' He started to laugh. And so I sat on the sofa all night long watching my beloved son endure something no human being, let alone a child, should ever have to endure. As dawn broke Billy sloped off to bed. I gently untied Paul who was in a half awake, half asleep daze and carried him to his bed. While Billy slept, Paul slept. Billy appeared to be at peace with himself but Paul moaned and whimpered from the pain of the blows.

Billy cooked some evil meals for us. One time he made a stew of beans and vegetables and tipped almost an entire pot of pepper into it. Then he forced Paul to eat it.

'Eat, you fucking brat, eat,' he snarled. Paul kept screaming and spitting the food out as Billy tried to spoon it into his mouth.

'You should be grateful I'm putting food into your mouth at all, you snivelling ...' He broke off mid-sentence because Paul had vomited all over his hand.

Then he started punching Paul. Paul retreated into himself, in too much pain to cry. When Billy went out, carefully locking the front door behind him, Paul sat on the sofa in obvious agony. I looked across the room at him, too distraught to touch him in case picking him up hurt him more. Cher was singing 'Believe' on the TV. It was his favourite song and he was trying to sing along to it but his mouth was too bruised and bloody to allow any sound to come out. I sat on the floor and put my head in my hands. I was leaning against the door to the balcony and suddenly it opened. Billy usually checked and double-checked to make sure that that door was locked too but somehow he'd overlooked it today. I decided it was a sign. We wouldn't get another chance. He'd moved in with us three months ago but our time in captivity felt longer than three decades. I stood on the balcony and peered over the side. The flat was on the first floor. I considered jumping with Paul in my arms but thought it was too risky. Newspaper headlines flashed through my mind after the two of us were discovered flattened and blood-spattered on the pavement below. 'Mum and son in tragic suicide pact.' I decided I wanted to live. On the left-hand side of the balcony was a drainpipe. It looked sturdy. I ran into the flat and like a mad woman threw Paul's coat on to him and told him to climb on to my back and put his arms firmly round my neck.

'We're going to be free soon, darling,' I said to him, panting with panic that Billy might walk back through the door at any moment. I climbed carefully over the balcony. Paul clung obediently to my back. Getting down was easier than I'd expected. I gripped the drainpipe and we slid down easily. Paul didn't make a sound: he was too surprised. As soon as my feet touched the ground I grabbed him and ran and ran.

8. FAILING TO STOP

I found us a cheap flat to rent in a different part of south London and for a while I laid low. I felt too paralysed to call friends. I got in touch with my mother, thanked her for alerting Social Services then tried to play the whole thing down.

'I was living with a violent guy but I saw sense and walked away. It's just Paul and me now and everything's going to be fine.'

'Thank goodness you're safe,' said my mother. 'I had a feeling that something terrible was going to happen to you.'

My mother wasn't wrong to worry, but she didn't know that having narrowly escaped a situation that was becoming life-threatening, I would go on to place myself in much more dangerous situations.

I was still utterly devoted to Paul but was in no fit state to look after him and provide the emotional guidance that every child deserves. I was far more damaged by Billy than I had been by Leroy. I had no one to turn to, no one to help me heal. I didn't want to see my family or my friends. Seeing familiar people was as painful as having an abscess pressed. If I could manage to get through the day without brushing against anyone who cared about me I could survive but if anyone tried to probe I was certain that abscess would burst, splattering pus on them and myself. Billy had left me feeling that I amounted to nothing more than an empty shell. I believed his threats that if I ever escaped he'd hunt me down and kill me and then he'd go round to my brother's flat and kill him before ending his spree by fatally stabbing my mother. I was terrified of a police officer tracking me down to break the tragic news that my mother and brother had been caught up in a Billy bloodbath.

What I didn't understand was that I needed a period of bereavement, a quiet, peaceful time in which I could painstakingly restore my shattered strength. Instead the oblivion of drugs beckoned. Once I was free from Billy I went back to using speed and ecstasy. I developed an appetite for base speed, which is ten times stronger than normal speed. I bought it in a wet, grainy paste and spent about £45 a week on the stuff. I felt constantly revved up like a motorbike with no open road to expend my energy on. I was awake for days on end and when I did finally sleep it was never for more than two or three hours. Taking speed made me feel normal and rational and human again. Ultimately it was the equivalent of jumping into an acid bath to soothe third degree burns but as a short term anaesthetic the drug worked well.

I lost interest in food and became even skinnier than I was before, which was gratifying. One of the advantages of taking drugs was that they blunted my eating disorder. When I wasn't using many drugs I was preoccupied with food. I pored over packets in supermarkets to check out the calories and measured every morsel that I swallowed. Stimulants like speed made food seem as appealing as a grey bowl of gruel and when my size eight jeans hung off me I jumped for joy. 'Maybe I could market the "tea-spoon of speed a day" diet or the "a rock of crack a day keeps the pounds away" diet,' I joked with the friends I sat in the pub with, people whose jeans were similarly wrinkled with space where flesh had once lain snug against the denim.

Crack had suddenly exploded on to London's drug scene. Billy had smoked it but not too many other people I knew. But now it was, it seemed, all the rage. Game, as ever, for new anaesthesia and with the novelty of ecstasy and speed wearing thin, I bought a £10 rock to share with friends. The love affair between me and the white, crystallised lump was instant. After inhaling the fumes for the first time I was irked that I was expected to share the stuff.

To those who have no wish to be chemically altered it's difficult to describe just what it is about the sudden euphoric rush, the sense of absolute confidence in your own invincibility and the (very) temporary filtering out of painful problems that crack offers. Wise people lead even, tranquil lives and decide to forgo that moment of euphoria because they understand only too well the jittery paranoia which trails in its wake, the compulsive picking off of invisible blemishes on the skin, the maddening imprint on the brain of the first joyful experience, which is never quite repeated. That taste which lingers deep in the DNA can literally drive users crazy when they can't get their hands on more.

Heroin, in clean, regular, measured doses, while horribly addictive, neither ages nor withers the heart, lungs, liver and the rest. But with cocaine there are the premature heart attacks and strokes which too many friends have succumbed to in their twenties and thirties. Cocaine fast-forwards your life – you can reach fifty while you're still thirty, or at least your vital organs can. Thirty-year-olds pant down the street with the damaged heart usually seen in people in their sixties and accident and emergency departments have been reporting an increase in this phenomenon of old hearts in young bodies amongst cocaine users. Of course none of this mattered to me. I jumped in head first and embraced the crack pipe like a long-lost lover. A friend of mine lived miserably with a myriad addictions for many years. Crack was the one he found most difficult to part from. He once said cheerfully to me: 'The only good thing about crack is that it brings you to your knees really quickly. If you sit in an Alcoholics Anonymous meeting a lot of people are in their fifties or sixties before alcohol brings them down. With crack it's a matter of months so there's a chance you can get out while you're still young and start again.'

I was twenty-one years old and generally started my day with a nice cup of tea – with a teaspoon of speed stirred into it. I tried to desist from smoking crack until later in the day. The fact that I was still using speed and ecstasy and cannabis alongside it slowed my habit down a bit and it wasn't until I reached my late twenties that my appetite for crack became truly ferocious. I dipped in and out of a heavy but not a classically addictive pattern of drug use over the next few years. I wasn't working and so had to confine my drug use to what I could afford out of my benefits. I made sure that Paul's needs were catered for first but I spent almost nothing on myself, surviving on economy pasta and cornflakes so that every possible penny could be spent on drugs.

When I used either cocaine or crack and speed together they blended into a dazzling, nervy high. My drug use affected my health. Partly because of the drugs and partly because I was barely eating I developed a sore throat so bad it felt as if I was ripping the skin off it every time I swallowed, accompanied by a high fever. My mother came to visit, took one look at me and called an ambulance. I was diagnosed with poisoned tonsils. As I lay in the hospital bed having the poison syringed out of my tonsils, I at last recognised that I had a problem. Overwhelmed with guilt for my failures as a parent, I resolved to do something about my drug problem and when I was released from hospital several days later, pumped full of antibiotics, I made enquiries about drug treatment programmes. The attempt was rather a half-hearted one, though. I opted for a day programme – it seemed more manageable than a residential option and it was the shortest one on offer. I had to put Paul, who was then four, into foster care while I did the programme and I missed him terribly.

'Mummy is poorly. I have to go into hospital so that they can make me better and then we'll be back together again.'

He looked at me dolefully, his big brown eyes searching my face for signs that I might be lying.

I didn't use drugs while I was doing the programme and looking back I suppose it did feel good to live without them for a while. But to have any sort of success you have to allow your mind to bend in the same direction as the philosophy of the programme. I felt as if my mind was bending in entirely the opposite direction, like a rogue banana in a bunch twisting away from the rest. I was intrigued by the other participants' confessions of their own drug use; I marvelled at the range of techniques which existed to get substances into the body.

There was a motley crew of people attending the programme: a few hardened heroin addicts who seemed determined to quit once and for all, a wealthy teenage girl from Chelsea whose parents had forced her to attend because they discovered she was taking a few ecstasy pills at weekends and felt she was sliding dangerously towards Class A drugs, two businessmen who were trying to beat their addiction to cocaine. One had had a minor, cocaine-induced heart attack and the other was no longer able to work effectively because he was running to the bathroom of the American bank where he worked to snort more and more lines of coke.

I listened with interest to the heroin addicts describing their love affair with the drug and how it had dragged them down. That sounded like a very serious-minded kind of addiction and I wondered if I would one day experience it myself. I empathised with the coke addicts. My liking for stimulants was similar to theirs. We all had the urge to constantly buzz, buzz, buzz. Without an electric current perpetually shooting through us we didn't feel properly alive. As for the ecstasy girl, I was silently scornful of her presence on the programme. Gulping down a handful of ecstasy pills a few nights a week wasn't an addiction as far as I was concerned.

The people in charge of the day programme talked to us about triggers for our drug use, problems in our childhoods, ways to find substitutes for chemical pleasure.

I listened and nodded but I wasn't interested in becoming a sober grown-up. By the end of the first week I was bored stiff. I found different mind games to play with myself to try and make the time pass more quickly – counting every single hair on my left forearm, swinging my legs until I was worn out, manufacturing large numbers of yawns and trying to outyawn my previous personal best in each session.

I'm sure that for the participants who were motivated to stop using drugs the programme worked well but I wasn't ready to stop. I felt I'd hardly started with my drug-using career. I was missing Paul terribly and I missed drugs almost as much. The second we were released from the programme, I raced back to both. I was like a car without brakes. All I could do was hurtle onwards, assuming that eventually I would crash into a wall and combust.

9. THE £200 RIBENA DRINK

For a few weeks I tried to be disciplined about the drugs. Living with a body free of chemicals while I attended the day programme wasn't as unbearable as I'd thought it would be. But once I left I was surrounded by friends who took drugs and I slid back into my old ways. Then the worst thing for a heavy drug user happened – I received a payout of £45,000 in compensation for the accident I'd had when I was twelve. The compensation claim was settled soon after the accident. The position of the driver on the wrong side of the road and the accounts from witnesses meant that there were no arguments about the fact that the driver was at fault. However, haggling over the precise amount I would receive and when I would receive it was another matter and involved almost a decade of on-off negotiations between lawyers and insurance companies. At the back of my mind I knew that some day I would receive a large sum of money but I never knew exactly when it was going to arrive.

I was happy when the cheque finally did appear but not overjoyed. It was too large an amount of money for me to comprehend and I was a little scared of it. I had been learning to drive and decided I would take some more lessons, try to pass my driving test and then buy myself a car. I bought lots of clothes and toys for Paul and a mobile phone for me. It was bliss no longer having to hunt for a phone box every time I wanted to make a call.

Alas, I never got round to taking driving lessons and passing my test. I decided that I would buy drugs and sell them on to friends, the theory being that that way my capital would remain intact and I could live off the interest. I bought from my own dealers but instead of selling the drugs on I ended up giving them away to friends and acquaintances. I'm ashamed to say that in a matter of months my payout was completely gone. I hated myself for having frittered the money away and decided I needed to make a fresh start yet again.

I tried to move away from the friends and dealers I spent most of my time with. I had to find a way to support us and instead of choosing something sensible, found my way to Soho. I reasoned that as it was evening work I could put Paul to bed and leave him with a babysitter and then devote myself to him during the hours of daylight.

Setting foot in Soho was love at first sight for me. It was like a pageant without end. A little hidden village of sleaze and fantasy that danced to a different beat than Leicester Square, Piccadilly Circus and the other parts of London's West End that cornered yet seemed to ignore it.

An organised type of anarchy made things run very smoothly in Soho. All the clubs were interlinked in one way or another and everybody knew everybody else's business. For the most part the police and Westminster Council left the sex industry to its own devices, intervening only intermittently to raid establishments operating illegally, pull out under-age girls or deport foreign women whose papers weren't in order. The characters who inhabited the area romped through the streets in unmanageable stilettos, indecent mini skirts and cleavage swaying for all to see, whatever the weather. The perpetual fancy dress of the place appealed to me. Putting myself on show was another way of escaping from myself.

My route into employment in Soho was via a small advert in the back of a local free newspaper. 'Hostesses wanted for gentleman's club. Good rates paid.' I phoned the number in the advert and was asked to turn up for an interview at a café on Wardour Street. So far, so respectable. I'd managed to cut down my drug use by sheer effort of will and without huge doses of speed had gone up to size ten so looked reasonably healthy. My hair at that time was long, undyed brown and curled down my back. I wore a tight lycra dress which left little to the imagination and six-inch stilettos for the interview. I sat on the bus in a long coat and a pair of trainers because it was impossible for me to walk more than fifty yards or so in the stilettos. As soon as I approached the café I took my coat off and switched my shoes.

I arrived at the café at the appointed time, 6 p.m. It was one of those places that didn't look very interested in selling food or drink. There were only a few curled-up sandwiches and dried-out currant buns in a solitary glass case on the counter and a big urn with a box of PG Tips next to it. It was like a film set of a café rather than the real thing.

'I've come for an interview about the hostess job,' I said hopefully to a bored older woman in a baggy T-shirt and black leggings with long, mousy hair coiled into a fat bun in the nape of her neck. She was sitting behind the counter reading the *Sun*.

'Bill!' she called out shrilly to a closed door at the back of the café.

A middle-aged man appeared, rubbing his eyes as if he'd just been woken up.

'Come this way, love.' He beckoned to me to follow him. My theory about the café just being some kind of front for something else seemed to be correct. He opened another door at the back of the shop and led me down a dank, slippery flight of steps into a gloomy basement.

'Welcome to Madame Mirabelle's. Now, you look like a girl with a bit of experience of life.' He raised one eyebrow knowingly at me. 'That's just the kind of girl we need here. Your job will be to sit with the customers, flirt with them, entertain them, get them to spend a fortune on our special brand of non-alcoholic cocktails and then if they pay all the club's charges they'll get a private dance in one of the booths from you. You get a cut of what each customer pays. How does that sound?'

I looked around at the decor – peeling black and red paint on the walls, two battered sofas – and inhaled the pungent odour of damp and sweat, overlaid with cheap air freshener.

The advert had said the hostesses were needed for a gentlemen's club. I had worried that the establishment might be too upmarket and that I would be out of my depth, rubbing shoulders with models and jet-setting businessmen. I knew there was no danger of bumping into either of those groups in this establishment.

'Yes, it sounds fine. I'll take it,' I said decisively.

'Excellent. Start tomorrow 5 p.m. See you then,' said Bill. 'Don't wear too many clothes.

I'd always loved dancing when I went clubbing and had sometimes, self-consciousness stripped away by ecstasy and speed, got up on stage and danced suggestively with friends. The prospect of dancing and being the centre of attention again thrilled me.

Shifts were 11 a.m. – 5 p.m. and 5 p.m. – 11 p.m. I tried to work double shifts wherever possible and that way managed to earn a reasonable amount of money. I didn't work weekends and devoted all my time then to Paul to compensate for my absences during the week.

Out of an average £400 bill the men were charged, we hostesses got paid around £125. It was always cash in hand, which suited me well. The hostesses were expected to stand in the doorway of the club (next door to the non-café café) and reel in unsuspecting males, usually tourists. Everything about us exuded sleazy sex, our three-quarters exposed breasts, our diaphanous short skirts and of course those fantasy-heeled stilettos.

The men's penises propelled them through the door, hardening with anticipation at the flashes of exposed flesh. Little did they know that the sexiest thing they were likely to get once they'd stepped over the threshold was a £200 Ribena cocktail – hostess clubs like this one didn't have licences to serve alcohol. Selling sex to the customers was strictly prohibited although sometimes when the manager was nowhere to be seen the doorman 'accidentally' turned off the CCTV cameras, which allowed hostesses to negotiate sex with a customer in one of the dancing booths for a separate fee.

I settled in straight away. A dapper man nicknamed Maltese Monty, who always wore a black suit, white shirt and trilby hat, looked after the hostesses, running to the shops to buy us sweets and cigarettes. His craggy, cheeky face reminded me of the late actor Sid James. He got along well with all the hostesses, was kind to us all and quickly became part of the fabric of my daily life in Soho.

After a couple of days there I began to understand the finely tuned sequence of events which began the moment a man walked along the street looking vaguely interested. Pouting in our scanty outfits we coaxed him over the threshold whispering: 'Private striptease. Five pounds.' What none of the men understood at this early stage was that there was a full stop between the words 'striptease' and 'five' and that sitting invisibly between those two words was the small matter of around £400 charges for a couple of non-alcoholic drinks with a vast VAT tax appended.

As soon as the men stepped inside, a CCTV camera winked at them. They were trapped. The threat of the wives they invariably had back home discovering where they'd been usually made them pay up, however flabbergasted they might be when they received the extortionate drinks bill.

While the men didn't have the option of drinking anything stronger than fruit juices, the hostesses all knocked back copious amounts of 2020 lager. It was only when we were at least slightly drunk that we could pose on the doorstep of Madame Mirabelle's and dance seductively for a generally repulsive group of men. Clubs like this depended on a subtle combination of honesty, deception and magnificent acting from the hostesses to succeed. Dramatic timing was also essential. If we missed our cue the men might realise before they'd ordered a drink that they were being conned and could march out without parting with any money.

These mysterious VAT charges increased twentyfold the cost of the drinks. There was a small notice on the wall just inside the entrance to the club stating without explanation that these charges would be made but our job was to wiggle and simper and make suggestive comments in such a way that the last thing on the men's minds was reading a notice in small print on the wall. We beckoned them to follow us into one of the secluded booths in the club. When they sat down the waitresses brought them menus but before they could study them we would point to one of the exotically named fruit cocktails like Hawaii Sunset (Ribena and orange juice), lean even closer to them so that they could feel our breath on their lips, our breasts resting against their arm and purr: 'I strongly recommend the Hawaii Sunset.'

With luck they barely glanced at the menu, where the VAT charges were once again written in small print. They assumed that a drink couldn't cost more than a few pounds and in a state of at least semi-arousal preferred to look down our cleavage than to study the menu at any great length.

The chit-chat stage lasted for approximately ten minutes and involved a series of inane exchanges between us hostesses and the customers. Dangerous subjects like the customers' wives and children were never mentioned. Instead we stuck to safe areas like whether they had been sightseeing in London if they were tourists, or if they were worn out from back to back business meetings if they weren't, if they'd been to any nice bars or restaurants in London's West End. And on and on, giggling, pretending to be very stupid and showing as much leg and breast as possible to maximise their arousal. Maintaining eye contact was very important because it stopped them noticing any of the written clues about the VAT charges.

After ten minutes the waitress would glide into the booth with the bill. If it was left any longer the man might start to twitch with anxiety and suspicion, any shorter and he might feel he'd been conned out of his time with his hostess.

Sometimes customers wept or turned a clammy shade of grey as if they were about to have a cardiac arrest when they were presented with the bill. I sat impassively while they gasped over the bill, telling myself that that part of their experience in a sleazy Soho club was nothing to do with me. The waitresses brought the menus, the drinks and the bill to the men while the job of the hostesses was to get men over the threshold and keep them inside spending money for as long as possible. It was similar to the division of labour between maids and prostitutes who worked in flats. The waitresses wrote the bills by hand and the only acceptable form of payment was cash. Around half of the men paid enough of their bill, after varying degrees of protest, to get a private striptease. If the men paid the whole or even three quarters of their bill we were overjoyed and they received their private strip-tease without a quibble. If they insisted that they could only afford to pay half they would still get the dance if the club was quiet. But if they said they couldn't even afford half of the bill the waitress summoned Sanjay, a tall, athletic, young Indian man who was the club's enforcer.

He had a gentle nature but a deadly acting ability which equalled that of Shakespearean thespians when it came to forcing gullible men to settle £400 drinks bills. With his soft, peaceful features and demeanour, he would have been more at home meditating on a beach in Goa. He could coat himself with a tough, impenetrable varnish, though, when it came to forcing unsavoury men in Soho to pay crazily inflated drinks bills.

At times I and the other hostesses were verbally abused by the customers. 'Show us your tits, then, you fat old tart, if you know what's good for you,' and similarly charmless lines were part of some of the men's repertoires. With the men who insulted us I felt that their frantic reaction to the bill seemed like justice for the way they treated us. Usually they gasped something along the lines of: 'I don't have that sort of money in my bank account. I don't know what to do. My wife must never find out I've been in this place.'

At that point the waitress listening to this tale of woe would summon Sanjay over and he would boom at the man. 'I'm afraid this kind of excuse simply won't wash. We very strictly abide by the letter of the law here.' He pointed to a dark hole in the ceiling and told the lie that always unnerved customers more than anything else.

'In that hole we have placed a concealed CCTV camera. It is imperative in an establishment like this one that we gather that kind of evidence both for the protection of customers and staff. Should we ever need to take steps to launch legal proceedings against non-paying clients it is invaluable that we have that kind of legal backup.'

His face remained grave and inscrutable while he delivered this speech. Sometimes I and one of the other hostesses hid in one of the booths where private dances were performed for men who paid their bills, and there we would guffaw silently, bent double with the hilarity of Sanjay's impeccable oratory and the men's sweaty fright.

If the men hadn't been abusive I was relieved when they managed to pay enough to earn themselves a dance. I didn't mind seeing them conned but felt it was only right and proper that there should be some sort of consolation for the sting they had been caught up in.

Most of the girls who worked at the club were English although there were a few young Eastern European women who wanted to earn as much money as possible as fast as they could to send home to their families. They were very focused and once they'd reached their financial targets they got out and went home, often building a new family home or setting up a respectable business with the proceeds of their expedition into London's sexual under-world. While there were moments of camaraderie, there was also intense rivalry between the hostesses. We were all there for the same reason. I was aware that spending too long in Soho would pull me down just as my previous experiences had and admired the Eastern European women for planning their exit as soon as they'd arrived.

Almost as soon as I began working there I began drinking heavily to help me cope with the customers. I still used ecstasy at the weekends when I wasn't working but apart from the alcohol didn't use drugs while I worked in Soho. Bizzarely I rarely seemed to suffer any ill effects from my heavy drinking.

London's sex square mile chews up those who work in it and then spits them out for newer, younger, firmer models who can better sate the relentless appetite for fresh faces and flesh. Like the Eastern European women my plan was to stay long enough to benefit handsomely on a financial and personal level but not long enough to disappear into the mincer of young women that hid in every establishment in the rundown, crowded streets of London's red light district.

Some of the hostess clubs were raided by the police and closed down. I was lucky to escape almost unscathed from police investigations. There was only one occasion when

I thought I wasn't going to be able to avoid trouble. One fearless customer stormed out when presented with the bill and called the police. All of us were arrested and held at Marylebone Police Station for twelve hours. I was terrified but in the end they let us go without pressing charges.

Although I didn't plan to stay long in Soho I grew to love being there more and more. Sanjay and I started having a relationship. I called him my 'beautiful Indian god'. Gypsy women sometimes came to the door of the club selling revealing lacy outfits for the hostesses. Sanjay bought me several of them.

'You look fantastic in these "not there" outfits and the better you look the more money you can take home, isn't that right?' He had that impeccable way of speaking English that well-educated Indians had.

He came from a town at the foot of the Himalayas called Dehra Dun and had attended an eminent public school there called The Doon School. He told me that his father was a diplomat and his mother was a lecturer in anthropology.

'My parents sent me to England to broaden my horizons now that I've completed my university studies. They think I've taken a job in the University of London library. I'm broadening my horizons in a way my parents couldn't envisage in their wildest dreams – or nightmares.' He smiled sadly. 'Mind you, Soho might make an interesting anthropological study for my mother. One day I'll take you away from this place. We'll go and stay in my parents' villa in Dehra Dun,' he said. 'We can take a trip up into the mountains. The Himalayas are the only place on earth where I fully appreciate my true position in the vastness of the universe. A minute, insignificant speck. When I sit in the mountains gazing out at the world and understanding how I fit into it I get the most incredible sense of peace wash over me. In those moments it doesn't matter whether I continue to live or not. Death, breathing, everything, becomes an irrelevance.'

'I would love that, Sanjay,' I told him. 'I've never travelled outside Europe and I would very much like to see the world and understand it a bit better. I think that everything I've done with my life so far has been because I haven't felt that I belong properly in the world. All I want is to be a part of things.'

'We'll go,' he whispered, kissing me tenderly. 'We'll get out of this grasping, self-seeking shithole which is Soho where everybody's eyes are cast downwards in search of baser and baser objectives. And then we can lift our eyes and breathe in the best of the world. I'm tired of sinking with the worst of it.'

I decided it was best to keep quiet about my passion for Soho at that moment. The things Sanjay hated most about the place were the things I loved. I loved being desired by Sanjay, I loved being able to perch precariously in the doorway of Madame Mirabelle's and entice men down the grubby stairs into the grim basement simply by projecting a fantasy for them. I even loved Soho's crazed characters: Shouting Man who just walked up and down the parallel streets shouting peaceably at nothing and no one in particular, and Grey Man, a scruffy man with a heroin habit who strode purposefully in a square of Soho streets all day and most of the night. I don't know if Sanjay ever made it back to the Himalayas. I was shocked to bump into him years later at the same homeless hostel that I was staying in. He was as sunken and diminished by heroin and crack as the rest of us were. I was appalled. I had always believed that he was different and that he would somehow manage to be of that world without being in it. But the more uneasy Sanjay became with the world of Soho, the more I enjoyed it.

One time one of the sprauncier clubs phoned up Madame Mirabelle's and said they urgently needed a girl to perform a striptease for a group of Japanese tourists who had just descended on them.

'We've got one girl too hung over to perform, another off sick with food poisoning and a third who's booked the afternoon off to have an abortion. We're really, really short staffed.'

'Could you go?' Sanjay asked.

'Of course,' I said, throwing a sparkly cardigan over my gaping, halternecked mini dress.

I put my heart and soul into the dance, basking in the attention and the feeling that I was a beautiful and desirable creature. But while I was performing I knew that I was on the cusp of change, that this perfect life of being panted after by scores of men, of having Sanjay, of going home every night with a few hundred pounds in my pocket, was a golden moment, briefly freeze-framed before a sharp descent.

I spent almost a year in Soho but then like everything else I'd tried the novelty faded. The same things that had once glinted brightly and drawn me to them now seemed dull and tarnished. I felt the familiar urge to move on although I didn't have anything in particular to move on to. When I left I ended my relationship with Sanjay. He was devastated. He'd told me that I was his 'soulmate' and that we were destined to be together forever. I was trapped on a one-way conveyer belt and all I could do was endlessly move on. Whenever I did this I left everything from my most recent life behind, apart from Paul of course, believing that that was the only way I could start afresh.

It reminded me of when I was at school and kept making a mess of my sums. I scribbled through the wrong answers and turned over to the next blank page to start the sums again in my exercise book. But however many times on however many new pieces of paper I tried again I continued to mess my sums up in the same way. The new pieces of paper didn't help me understand how to do the sums any better and I was too shy and stubborn to ask the teacher for guidance. I didn't realise as a child that there was no point in me continually starting again until I could either decipher for myself where I had gone wrong the last time or get someone else to explain and interpret my mistakes to stop me repeating them. When I left Soho I understood this no better than I had as a child, grinding my teeth over my repeated failure to divide 483 by fourteen.

10. OTHER PEOPLE'S MONEY

The people I mixed with hovered unhappily on the fringes of society. I met them in the pubs I sat in, at the down-at-heel clubs where I gulped handfuls of ecstasy pills and in the queue at my local social security office. The government rhetoric about alleviating poverty and ensuring that everyone had a stake in society hadn't touched the lives of the people I consorted with. Not for them the smooth trajectory of a focused education at a well-ordered school, followed by a university degree, a well paid, stable job, a mortgage, a partner and a couple of lucky children who would slot into the same grooves in the tramlines as they had, embarking on a journey which involved long-term planning and never taking your eye off the ball.

What distinguished me and my friends from this middle-class and aspirational working-class cohort was that none of us had a plan. Our existence was hand to mouth. We either hadn't been taught or couldn't bear to look down the long road which was the future. Many but not all of us came from troubled homes with shocking rates of emotional illiteracy, from backgrounds of lovelessness and violence, homes where little living, breathing importance was given to education and where life aspirations were terribly low. Mostly we thought we didn't deserve a better life, and those who inhabited that clean, pleasant space in the polluted sea of existence wouldn't want us in their club even if we knocked on the door politely. So what was left was to take a contrary, hurt pride in being outsiders, with very different methods of income generation. We couldn't find ourselves so instead we lost ourselves the only way we knew, using the blunt instrument of drugs and alcohol.

In our world a fair bit of moneyless bartering went on. Shoplifted goods were swapped for drugs, sex was swapped for drugs and stolen cheque books were swapped for drugs. There was money too in our alternative economy, cash in hand earned from occasional days of labouring on building sites, from loan sharks, social security money, money acquired in muggings. But this money never touched the ground and certainly never lay idly in bank accounts. It whizzed from hand to hand and however much of it there was it was never enough.

And so it was easy to slip into working for a group of Nigerian fraudsters. A couple of my pubbing, clubbing friends knew them and said they were looking for an attractive young woman who could 'do respectable' to front their operation, fleecing the accounts of the innocent in building societies around London

Fraud sounded so much more sophisticated than shoplifting. I thought of Clyde's Bonnie and Bill Sykes' Nancy. These women weren't bad. They were risk takers like me. The training was minimal. They always worked with women who walked into building societies dressed expensively but not brashly, who put on their best Queen's English voice and drew money out of the accounts of people whose cheque books, pass books and cards were newly stolen. The Nigerians were working with a postman who was stealing people's new cheque books and cards before they ever received them, which gave us more time before the missing money was noticed.

I wouldn't have dreamed of mugging an old lady for her pension but this was different. Banks and building societies fleeced their customers, they were insured against such losses and reimbursed those whose accounts were plundered. The way I saw it nobody lost out. The thought of walking into a building society pretending to be someone else didn't scare me. It was a new way to hide from myself.

I was taken to a flat in Balham by Bill, the friend who had told me that a gang of cheque book fraudsters was looking for a front woman. He introduced me to three taciturn Nigerian men, dressed expensively in leather jackets and frighteningly shiny black shoes. Then he disappeared. I felt slightly uneasy. The men gave off a hostile vibe and barely spoke to me.

The flat was bare but had piles of documents everywhere. It looked as if it was used as an office rather than as living quarters.

'Please sit down,' said one of the men, gesturing to me to join the rest of them at a battered wooden table.

'What you have to do is go up to the counter, draw out however much money we tell you to draw out and walk away calmly. Are you in or out?' said the tallest man, who appeared to be the leader. He told me his name was Tim but I heard the other men call him Amara.

I nodded hesitantly. None of them smiled back. They began talking in a language I didn't understand and in fact they generally excluded me from their conversations this way. All of them were very focused on the task in hand. They had worked out exactly where the loopholes in the system were and the various ways to wriggle through them. They approached their work as meticulously as an MI5 operative.

Paul had started school and I told them I could only work until around 2.30 p.m. as I had to make sure I was at the school gates promptly to collect him.

'No problem,' said Amara. 'We'll drop you off at your boy's school. It's important that you draw money out during housewife hours, you'll attract less attention to yourself that way.'

One of the men rifled through a pile of papers and produced a handful of building society pass books. Then he produced a small, bright light that he shone on to the pass books to reveal the holder's signature.

'OK, see this signature, you need to practise and practise it until it becomes your own. When you sign for the withdrawal of the money you mustn't hesitate even for a split second or all will be lost. Understand?'

I nodded, trying to look as streetwise as possible. I felt they considered me to be an idiot and I was determined to prove them wrong.

I did well at forging the signatures and Amara nodded his approval to me.

He looked me up and down and put his hand in his pocket pulling out a bulging wallet.

'You can't walk into those places dressed in jeans, a tee-shirt and scruffy trainers,' he said. 'You need a uniform. This whole business is like being an actress in a play, right? You can't go on stage without your costume. Go out and buy yourself something designer. If you want to wear jeans get the best and make sure you've got a classy handbag and some tasteful rich-housewife make-up. OK.'

He handed over £200 in well-worn £20 notes.

'OK, interview over, you can go home now. Buy yourself something decent with the cash. Write down your address on this piece of paper and we'll pick you up at 9.15 tomorrow morning.'

'That's great. Thanks so much, Tim, I'll see you tomorrow.'

I was glad to get out of the flat. I had a queasy feeling that all three of them were laughing at me behind my back. The men picked me up the following morning. I had bought some designer jeans, a pair of suede boots and a silk shirt.

'Nice gear, you look just right,' said Amara, 'Jump in.'

They had an anonymous-looking Honda, not too flash and not too battered. And again they said little to me but talked animatedly amongst themselves. I felt the same dirty feelings wash over me as the first time I had sex for money, just before I was fifteen. But what kept me going then was the same thing that kept me going now. I was going to walk away with money. I had a sense that these men were part of a much bigger network of cheque book and card fraud but I was only given information on a 'need to know' basis and anything other than which building societies we were going to raid was kept from me.

I strolled into a building society in Croydon, clutching my passbook. My name was Deborah Yardley with a curly flourish in the tail of the final 'y'.

Her account contained almost £20,000 according to her stolen passbook. I felt slightly nervous but at the same time my heart and my stomach fluttered pleasantly with the exciting newness of it all.

'Can I help you?' said the beaming cashier. I obviously looked very Deborah Yardley-like as she didn't seem to suspect a thing.

'Could I withdraw £500, please?' I said.

'Certainly, Mrs Yardley. Could you sign here for it, please?'

I signed perfectly.

The cashier handed over £500 in £20 notes.

'Have a nice day,' she said with a smile. 'Next please.'

I walked out slowly with the money and handed it to Amara.

He nodded approvingly.

As promised I was dropped off outside the gates of Paul's school at 3.30 p.m. There were a couple of other young women who Amara had also recruited and they too had young children to collect from school. It was the ultimate in child-friendly, flexible working.

I had played the role of the sober middle-class mum well and never once did I encounter a cashier who so much as raised an eyebrow at me.

Fortunately frauds rarely last forever. We were caught in Wembley one rainy morning very soon afterwards. I was sitting in the Honda with Amara and a couple of the other women. We were waiting for another car to pull up alongside us containing some of Amara's friends. But as it pulled up four police cars surrounded both of our vehicles and arrested us all. I was frantic, but not so much because I feared arrest. I had no documents of any description on me and thought that the police wouldn't be able to prove anything because I hadn't touched the documents in the other car, so there was no fingerprint trail on them leading back to me.

We were taken down to the local police station. I was allowed to call a friend who collected Paul from school and said she'd hang on to him until I could get back.

I had never been in a police cell before and the whole process of being booked in by two surly, burly officers terrified me. I said nothing.

One of the officers explained that they were going to search my house and that if they found nothing incriminating I and the other two women would be released the next morning. I was brought some stringy bits of beef and processed mashed potato for supper but felt too churned up to eat.

I spent an anxious night tossing and turning on the hard mattress in a cell painted a sickly pastel shade of yellow. The following morning a police officer unlocked my cell with the biggest bunch of keys I'd ever seen.

'You three ladies can all scarper, nothing was found at your addresses.' I looked at him incredulously.

'Go on, hop it, unless you want to spend another night at the Ritz.'

I grabbed my coat and ran out of the police station. It had been raining all night but it had stopped about five minutes before I was released. I took it as a sign that today the world, God or whatever determined my fate, was on my side. The sun shone fiercely, making the wet pavements sparkle. It was exhilarating to be free and to feel the fresh air stroke my face. I raced home. I would have just enough time for a quick shower and to cover up the traces of the police search before it was time to collect Paul from school. I felt very blessed.

11. THE CRASH THAT MADE A BABY

Despite my vow to stay away from men after my experience with Billy, I allowed Darren to literally crash into my life. Darren drove into the back of my car one day and after my initial annoyance I was smitten. He was a young, extremely attractive black man with the biggest smile I had ever seen. I was with a female friend and we both jumped out the car, hands on hips, not prepared to be convinced by any sort of feeble excuse he might have been about to offer.

'I'm so sorry,' he said, grinning, not looking at all sorry and holding his hands up in a 'don't verbally beat me up' gesture. 'I was miles away, daydreaming as usual, entirely my fault. But the lucky thing is I work in a garage.' He took out a scrap of paper and wrote his phone number down on it.

'My name's Darren. Just call me up any time and I'll fix the damage for you – free of charge, obviously.'

'Thank you, Darren, I'll definitely be in touch,' I said, trying to sound icy but grinning instead.

He mended the car beautifully and somehow we kept finding reasons to call each other. He wasn't a cruel psychopath or a crazed addict. In fact, he was a normal man with a delightful family who instantly welcomed me into their midst. Darren's fatal flaw was his love of women, not just one or two but many different ones. But that was something I wasn't aware of in the early days.

I was excited to be with him and felt that it was one of the first right decisions that I'd made in my life. I temporarily lost interest in drugs because he didn't use them. We began a relationship swiftly. We were both strongly attracted to each other and he was very funny. Any man who could make me laugh out loud appealed to me enormously. He used to pull comical faces and make witty comments about everyday situations. He was also very affectionate and would often cuddle me and make me feel secure. I was renting a flat in Balham with Paul and he moved in with me after a few weeks. He was very good to Paul, who was seven, and spent a lot of time playing with him and talking to him.

I was still in my clubbing phase and liked nothing better than to book a babysitter and dance the night away in a club, downing ecstasy, speed and sometimes cocaine or ketamine. Darren was not as wild as me. He came along with me to clubs but wasn't interested in taking drugs. After a few hours he was ready to leave but I was always enjoying myself far too much to go home.

After nine months together things were still going well. My self-esteem remained very low and it was a boost to me to have such an attractive man on my arm. Both of us were very keen on the idea of family life. We talked about trying for a baby and soon afterwards I got pregnant. We were both overjoyed and I had a very different experience of pregnancy with Darren from the one I'd had with Leroy. Darren was excited about the baby all the way through and came along to my scans and ante-natal appointments with me. As soon as I found out I was pregnant I stopped drinking and taking drugs completely. I loved going clubbing and found it hard just staying in in the evening while Darren went out with friends.

I had a trouble-free pregnancy but loathed putting weight on. Towards the end the only thing that fitted me was a baggy tracksuit of Darren's.

I vowed to embark on an extreme diet the moment the baby popped out.

Although I had always dreamed of living a 'normal' life with a partner and children I found being cooped up in the house for much of the time very claustrophobic and longed to return to my wilder days. During my pregnancy I got to know Darren's family. I loved going round there to visit with Darren and Paul. Darren's mother Stella played a key role in making the house a warm, happy and welcoming place.

When we tapped on her heavy door knocker I smiled and thought to myself: 'This is what proper families do.'

Once inside her big, child-filled house, I walked into another world. The rows of pairs of little shoes in the hallway and the happy shrieks of children alerted you before you'd even stepped over the threshold that this was a house of and for children. Food and warmth and endless conversations filled Stella's home. Her two youngest children still lived at home but there were usually another five or six passing through: cousins on extended sleepovers, school friends drawn into the warmth, neighbours. Any small child who wandered through the kitchen was scooped up and hugged and kissed by Stella. Whenever any toddler reached the age of three or four, he or she was given the name 'Munch Munch' by Stella. Once they started school the nickname slipped away, only to be revived when the next child reached that age. Stella and her four daughters, two in their twenties, two in their late teens, spent a lot of time at her home, although they'd all officially moved out. When they weren't cooking, cleaning or tidying up, they chatted around her big kitchen table sipping tea or coffee.

Stella, the matriarch, was a slim woman of medium height, with dreadlocks nestling neatly in the nape of her neck, tied in a red band. Her patience with all the children who came and went and those who stayed permanently was extraordinary. She gave and gave and gave of herself. I loved her dearly for welcoming me without reservation. All Darren's family were very excited about the fact that I was pregnant and assailed me with questions.

'How did your last appointment go? Are you eating properly? Must be a boy judging by the way that baby's lying, take it easy, we women have it tough, take the weight off your feet while you can.' I enjoyed being the centre of attention.

I was at home by myself when my contractions started. I called Darren calmly and he raced home. He seemed more panicked about the whole thing than me.

'Come on, jump in the car, we haven't got a moment to lose. They say that second babies come more quickly, don't they,' he said.

'I'm sure we've still got a bit of time,' I said. 'My waters haven't broken yet.'

My contractions were becoming closer together and more intense. Darren bundled me into the car and drove at top speed to get to the hospital, screeching round corners and jumping red lights. I felt like an extra in *Top Gear*. During the journey the pain got so bad that I started groaning and crying. By the time we arrived at the hospital I could barely walk. Somehow I managed to get up to the labour ward supported by Darren. My waters still hadn't broken so the midwife broke them for me with a device that looked like a knitting needle. I managed to get through labour with just gas and air. At one point they lost the baby's heartbeat. It had never occurred to me that anything might go wrong and suddenly I was terrified.

'Don't let me lose my baby, please,' I gasped between contractions. But thankfully the midwife found the heartbeat again. She had momentarily lost it because the baby was travelling so fast. Just when I thought I couldn't bear another second of pain a beautiful baby girl popped out and began to cry. The entire labour had lasted just three and a half hours. The midwife wiped her over, wrapped her up and handed her to Darren. He stood cradling her for several minutes. He seemed to be in some kind of a daze and had tears in his eyes.

'Isn't she beautiful, Rhea?'

I nodded, overwhelmed by the rush of emotions which follow birth: euphoria, relief, exhaustion and also joy that Darren was so involved and that the baby meant so much to him.

'Aren't you going to let mum have a hold of her?' asked the midwife, laughing. Darren clasped her tightly. He looked as if he was never going to relinquish his grip on her.

We decided to call the baby Keira and the following day we took her home. She was a beautiful cuddly baby and both of us adored her. On paper I had the kind of stability I'd dreamed of as a child but somehow every dream I attained evaporated mirage-like when it became a reality. After Keira was born, Darren seemed more distracted than usual. I was terrified that he was having an affair. My self-esteem had plummeted even lower than usual. I was finding it hard to shift my post-baby weight despite inflicting a diet of fruit, salad and black coffee on myself. I was tied to a domestic life which I found increasingly unappealing.

Darren began disappearing without explanation for hours on end, sometimes overnight.

'I know you're having an affair, Darren, please don't lie to me, I can't bear it,' I screamed at him at increasingly regular intervals. At first he denied it but later on when he was absent more and more often there seemed little point in him bothering to pretend.

Our rows became more and more frequent and I spent hours on end sobbing and feeling wretched about the sum of my existence, which consisted of cooking, cleaning and caring for two children.

I had really believed that my relationship with Darren would last forever and that we would grow old together walking monogamously into the sunset. Above all I felt terribly hurt at the loss of what the relationship represented. But out of some recess in my mind that I didn't know existed I found some strength. I decided that if things with Darren weren't going to last I needed to find a way to support myself and the children. I was twenty-three years old but had never had a real job. Thinking about it made me feel quite ashamed. I had always been interested in hair and had developed an aptitude for braiding the hair of friends and family. I cold-called a few hair salons and secured an apprenticeship at one.

Suddenly I felt better. I was gaining an identity beyond being a mother of two and partner to the increasingly unreliable Darren. Working in the salon made me realise how unhappy I was at home. I started cutting my long, brown hair shorter and shorter in a bid to reinvent myself. At the salon I was taught the basics of colouring, cutting and styling hair. I loved having a job and it gave me satisfaction to transform the appearance of a woman who came in looking tired and dowdy into a younger, brighter version of herself. I loved the environment of the salon, the warmth of the soapy water which washed clients' hair and the hot buzz of the hairdryers, the almond blossom scent of the shampoos and conditioners, the predominantly female chatter. The work was physically demanding but having a job to go to made me feel very secure.

For the next five years I supported myself and the children by working, sometimes intermittently, in a variety of different hair salons across London.

I managed to fit a lot of my work around collecting Paul from school and arranged childcare for Keira. Having a job and being needed in the salon boosted my self-esteem. One night I plucked up the courage to confront Darren about the shortcomings of our relationship. Keira was fifteen months old and was a bright and inquisitive little girl.

'Things aren't going to get any better than this, are they?' I said, trying to control the rage in my voice. 'I want you to leave, Darren. I'm going to find a new place to live and I'm taking the children with me.'

He looked stunned. I think he expected that however he behaved I would be there, waiting faithfully in the background.

He said little but began to pack his bags.

'I'll go back to live at my mum's,' he said sheepishly.

He seemed upset, as of course was I. In fact the pain for me was immeasurable. Almost as bad as the loss of Darren was the sense of personal failure. Another relationship with a man gone bad, another rejection, more feelings of bereavement. I wondered if things would ever go right. I felt emotionally minced by the experience. Two weeks after he left I moved out too to a new flat in another part of south London.

I wanted to make a fresh start but the siren call of drugs was beckoning me back. I became an expert, or so I thought, at concealing all traces of my drug use from my children. I loved them more than ever but caring for them was hard. In different ways both needed all of me all of the time. I felt I had no one to lean on. Trying to achieve the normal life with them that I had craved since my own childhood seemed harder than scaling Everest. In the end normal was just too hard. For me, my life was like my kitchen, much tougher to keep clean and tidy and ordered than to allow it to descend into unwashed, jumbled chaos. I was still taking ecstasy pills and had befriended a lonely cocaine dealer called Bam who craved my company. I tried to restrict my drug use during the week but had an arrangement with Darren that both Paul and Keira would spend weekends with him at Stella's house. Darren remained a devoted father to Keira and a very good surrogate father to Paul too. After the initial acrimony between us faded we managed to be civilised towards each other for the sake of the children and at the time of writing this has remained the situation. Although Darren and I are no longer together we know each other very well and a strong bond exists between us. He refers to Keira as his 'princess'. I'm delighted that Keira has always had a father in her life, unlike Paul and me. When I watch Darren and Keira together I wonder how things would have turned out for me if I had had a father in my life when I was growing up.

After Darren and I split up I dropped the children off after school on Friday at Stella's house and collected them on Sunday evenings. All the hours in between were devoted to an entirely bacchanalian lifestyle. I had learnt in school about Bacchus – in ancient Rome he was the god of wine and giver of ecstasy. I had been impressed at the time that such a god existed, who took pleasure in abandoning himself to intoxication, and he'd stuck in my mind ever since. I partied in dingy squats, downing ecstasy and when I wasn't dancing or slumped in the chill-out room because my legs were about to give way I went to Bam's flat and hoovered up each line of cocaine as if it were my last moment on earth.

During the week I continued to work as a hairdresser. I regularly moved from one salon to the next before managers had time to notice that my mind wasn't entirely on the job because of my drug use. After a while the work bored me. It's hard to hide when you're a hairdresser flanked by unforgiving mirrors and watchful clients. Being attentive and friendly was an essential part of the job and with some of the more awkward clients, like the fifty-something woman who blamed her thinning hair on my washing and cutting techniques rather than acknowledging the truth of her post-menopausal self, I wanted to ram the hairdryer into their mouths to keep them quiet. I never did, of course.

'Yes, Mrs Frost, you've changed your mind about the colour you'd like. No problem, I'll just go and mix up a new lot. No, Mrs Hatfield, you don't look like a tufted elf with your new feather cut. I've done it just like the picture in the magazine that you told me to copy.' And so it went on, tedious demand after tedious demand. The hairdressing profession is full of drugs, particularly cocaine, and there were ample opportunities, when we disappeared into the back room to mix up colour or fetch towels, to snort a quick line. It made me feel more benign towards the clients, and their chatter about their children and their miserly bosses seemed less tiresome with coke than without it.

I moved through the next four years like this. The children remained my priority and I faithfully delivered them to and from school, clothed them, fed them and played with them but I felt increasingly at a loss in the world. The money I made from my hairdressing was enough to support the three of us but life felt empty and painful. I worried that I had brought two children into the world who might have exactly the same feelings as me, a bewilderment at being born and having to make sense of the world. These thoughts made me feel even more of a failure as a mother and as a human being. I had so wanted to fulfill the dream of happy families with Darren and the children. All those stock cube and washing powder adverts told me that this was the way we were supposed to live. The initial disappointment when the dream came crashing down didn't abate as time went by, it intensified.

My belief that things just happened to me and that I had no control over the fact that God had stamped my life card 'UNLUCKY' helped to propel me further towards the void. If I was doomed to be an out-of-control junkie there was nothing else for it except to become an out-of-control junkie, I reasoned. I had tried to ration my crack smoking to a weekend treat but by the time I was twenty-seven it had begun to encroach on weekdays. There was something liberating about letting go. It felt as if I had been desperately squeezing my bladder tighter and tighter because I couldn't find a toilet to pee in. After squeezing and clamping my legs together for all I was worth, it simply became impossible to hang on any longer. I really wanted to find the toilet but however hard I searched I couldn't find one. Eventually I released my metaphorical muscles and wet myself. Losing my dignity and drifting towards a dark place where the normal rules of behaviour no longer applied was a huge relief. I began to smoke crack every day.

12. FALLING WITH CRYSTAL

I had met a woman called Crystal at the Mason's Arms pub. Like me she was trying and failing to juggle an escalating drug habit with bringing up her daughter. She was damaged, as I was, and we instantly recognised that in each other. It drove us together like a pair of magnets. She looked appealingly dramatic: skinny with red hair and enormous blue eyes. Between us we looked after her children and mine, dropping them off into the normal world of school before losing ourselves with our crack pipes. She switched between laughter and rage unpredictably and I often felt that she was so brittle that just a little bit more anger or manic joy and she would snap, her vocal cords strewn all over the floor.

Life with Crystal started off so well. Without anything as explicit as having a conversation about it, we agreed to play house together. The posturing as a pair of ordinary inner-city mothers was both for our benefit and our children's. I moved into her flat, a nondescript two-bedroomed place in Clapham that, like us, was on the edge of chaos but somehow gave the appearance of being more ordered than it actually was. We hid the piles of dirty washing out of sight, managing to wash just enough clothes to ensure that we and the children had something clean to put on each day. We kept the kitchen worktops reasonably clear of food debris but the sink was always always cluttered with yesterday's dishes and by the time we'd fed the children the fridge was often bare, apart from a mouldering jar of chutney and some ancient pickled onions that bobbed around forlornly in the briny water like reproachful, disembodied eyeballs.

Both of us were determined that the three innocent, wide-eyed children we had between us wouldn't get to know about our passion for crack. It was as if the children had become our spouses whom we had to behave respectably in front of, to conceal the fact that we were conducting a clandestine, torrid affair. But we were being unfaithful not with a seductive human with smooth flesh and a captivating smile but with little white lumps of chemical pleasure. I doubted that the peasant farmers who grew coca plants and the impoverished communities of Bolivia and Colombia who placidly chewed the leaves to stave off hunger or altitude sickness had even the vaguest notion of the insatiable greed for money and an altered mind of those involved in the production, distribution and consumption of the drug. I'd experienced pangs of guilt when I read in a magazine once, while waiting at a doctor's surgery, that Colombia had vast numbers of internally displaced people as a result of the cocaine business. But when there's something you want very badly it's easy to mothball such anxieties in the corner of the brain cupboard.

Crack induces the most unnatural appetites in those who worship, adore and loathe it in equal measure. Occasionally, when I was scurrying around trying to find the final £1.50 I needed to buy a £10 rock, I thought of the young women from the coca-growing countries who gulped down condom-wrapped packages of cocaine so bulky that their throats were bruised for weeks afterwards. Once they'd swallowed to order they flew into first world countries with every cell of their body stiff with the double fear of arrest and internal explosion. Like the coca leaf chewers, they had no sense of the madness surrounding the drug in the crack houses of London and other western cities. And like the dealers on the streets, they were peripheral figures in the money-making process, standing at the bottom of the dirty pile of people involved in this business with arms outstretched to catch the few drips of money the big men allowed to trickle into their hands. Mostly I tried not to think about the bigger picture. Instead I told myself that I didn't have a problem with crack, that life was tough, so I deserved to give myself a few little treats, and that I might stop using tomorrow or next week: the usual distorted drivel which characterises the rationale of an addict.

'C'mon, you two,' I called out again to Paul and Keira one morning, but they slumbered on. For the last ten minutes I had been trying to sound stern about them missing school if they didn't wake up. Crystal was mirroring my tone with her daughter Anya but none of them stirred.

Eventually all three kids appeared in the kitchen and sleepwalked their way through bowls of cornflakes. As we got ready to leave the house, they had the same dishevelled look as our lives had. Just about present and correct at first glance but on further inspection rather absent.

'Why wouldn't you let me sleep on, Mum?' mumbled Keira, who was four by this time, as I held her hand on the walk to school. She gazed accusingly at me through heavy-lidded eyes.

'Because, darling, it's very important for you to go to school and learn how to write all your letters beautifully. And once you can read you can read me bedtime stories instead of me reading them to you.'

The prospect of reading me stories appealed to her and her drowsy eyes opened slightly wider. I scooped her up into my arms and hugged her tightly. She was so small and soft and honest. Delivering her, Paul and Anya to school meant that the day was getting one step nearer towards smoking crack. I was still working as a hair-dresser but only part-time and did a mixture of days and evenings – a few times a week the salon I worked at offered late night opening up to 10 p.m. As I waved the children off – Keira was in her first year at primary school and Paul in his final year – the anticipation of the intense pleasure to come and the enormous guilt drenched me in equal measure.

Crystal and I had arranged to go to the supermarket to stock up on bread, milk, pasta and frozen peas, our children's staple diet and one which didn't make too much of a dent in our drugs budget.

'If only we could stock up on crack too,' I wanted to say, but of course didn't. Crystal was probably thinking the same thing but she didn't say anything either. As long as we played the game with each other that we were leading normal lives and didn't mention the C word, it was permissible to have the treat our hearts desired once we'd tucked the children up in bed and exchanged pleasantries with the babysitter.

I felt as if the straight world of parents and children and schools and supermarkets was like a slimming club and we were allowed to sneak a forbidden Mars Bar or two as long as our transgression didn't show up on the scales at the end of the week. But I knew that ultimately we wouldn't be able to balance the budget of our lives with our children with our whirlwind affair with crack.

The curious thing about crack was that while smoking it I felt euphoric and invincible and clear-sighted enough to vault over every life hurdle in my path. Yet I did nothing with those thoughts and feelings except plot ways to earn enough money for my next rock. Smoking crack was the ultimate mirage.

If Crystal and I hadn't had crack between us and binding us together we might have had a great deal to talk about – child rearing, ambitions, our respective philos-ophies of life – but we had no time to think about those things nor any interest in discussing them. We walked around Clapham in a desultory sort of way. Mentally I divided everyone we passed in the street into 'drug user' or 'non-drug user' categories.

The smackheads, as heroin users are referred to by their peers and rather disdainfully by crackheads, who consider themselves a notch above them in social standing, were always easy to spot. They were generally underweight; and I rarely saw fat heroin addicts. Apart from the empty space where there should have been body fat, heroin addicts were easy to spot because their skin had a particular dead, waxy quality to it, a peculiar hue of yellow and grey. They had hollow spaces under their cheekbones, blackened or missing teeth and a tormented and/or sleepy look in their eyes, depending on whether they had just used or were starting to withdraw.

The crackheads were more difficult to spot. Sometimes they too were skinny, but it depended on whether their habit was 'raging' or 'recreational'. Often, like Crystal and me, they were trying to keep up an appearance of normality. They would pass the 'normal' test if an unsuspecting passer-by glanced at them in the street but anyone who knew what to look for would see evidence of their ransacked mind in their restless faces, or notice the obsessive picking at imaginary scabs on their hands or forearms while they waited for a bus. And the paranoid tendencies – trying not to get too close to strangers in the street because they believed they were undercover police officers, aliens or social workers preparing to snatch their children.

As we walked along the high street I counted three smackheads, two possible speedballers and five crack-heads diluted by thirty-one 'normals'.

The unwritten rule between Crystal and me about not discussing our love for crack extended to other things too.

Although Crystal was very small and looked terribly fragile, with her porcelain skin and huge eyes, she was extraordinarily tough. She had a childlike self-belief which meant that she simply didn't see danger as I did. Generally she went to a local crack house and purchased a rock each for us to smoke. I had never had the courage to cross the threshold of those places. I imagined that crack houses were populated by incredibly violent men with guns concealed inside their jackets. I expected that at the very least one or more of these ferocious men would rape me at gunpoint and that it would be a race against time to hand my sweaty, crumpled £10 note over, grab my rock and bolt.

13. INITIATION

In fact my first experience inside a crack house was very different from my dark fantasy of it. Crystal had started going to crack houses during the day and I decided that sooner or later I would have to confront my fears and join her. It was a pity that I didn't choose more constructive fears to overcome than entering a crack house.

I called Crystal one morning. 'Hi, Crystal, what you up to?'

'Oh, hi, Rhea, I'm sitting in Pete's flat.' She sounded a bit giggly and maddeningly relaxed.

'Oh, OK if I pop down and join you for a while?' I tried to sound as if I didn't care whether I ventured into the crack house or not. As usual, neither of us had mentioned the C word. She gave me the address and I raced over there. I was working in a hair salon in Wandsworth at the time but wasn't due to start my afternoon/evening shift until 3 p.m. that day.

The place turned out to be an ordinary-looking council flat. It was on one of those prototype estates which I imagine predated the sixties council tower block building experiment in 'homes in the sky'. It was four rows of brick-built, four-storey-high flats around a quadrangle where cars could park and industrial-sized bins were stored. The flats were accessed by climbing a draughty stone staircase and then walking along an external walkway and simply knocking on the front door of the crack house. Media mythology talks about crack houses barricaded against the outside world with reinforced steel doors but in fact many crack houses on council estates don't look any different from the outside than the other flats. Crack houses are established very quickly and dismantled very quickly too, either as a result of a police raid or of a tenant who was initially willing to have their premises used for the selling and smoking of crack getting fed up and calling a halt to proceedings.

I thought the flat Crystal had told me to go to would look like the fortress of my imagination and that entry would only be granted by a man with a granite face poking me in the stomach with his gun to make sure I was a bona fide crackhead rather than a police plant or a rival dealer out to cause trouble. In fact, a gentle-looking, tall, skinny man called Pete opened the standard-issue council front door. His shoulder-length, greasy, brown hair flopped over his eyes and gaunt cheekbones. His skin had a horrible greenish-yellow tinge to it. It reminded me of the TV character The Incredible Hulk. I found out later that he injected heroin as well as smoking crack and realised that he was that ghoulish colour because he was suffering from hepatitis C, a potentially fatal virus rampant among injecting drug users.

He ushered me inside and I could see ten or eleven people crowded into his tiny living room, laughing and chatting. I was pleasantly surprised. If a man with scary-coloured skin was the worst thing I was going to encounter in a crack house, the whole thing would be an absolute breeze.

Crystal gave me a friendly wave and patted a spot next to her on the sofa that even an anorexic would have had problems squeezing into.

'Hi, Rhea, great to see you, come and join the party. I think we're all a little ahead of you.'

'Where's the dealer?' I asked, puzzled. This place with its bedraggled curtains, sticky carpet and unwashed bodies filling it up looked less and less like my vision of a crack house.

'He's sitting in the kitchen.' I balked at the prospect of venturing in there. Crystal sensed my unease.

'Should I go and score for you?' she whispered conspiratorially. I nodded gratefully. She whisked my £10 note out of my hand and bounded into the kitchen, closing the door behind her so I never got to see who the mysterious dealer was. Not seeing him added to his mystique.

Did dealers in crack houses have more ferocious DNA than those I knew who sold drugs on the street or in pubs, I wondered, as I inhaled deeply, greedily sucking up all the fumes from my pipe. I felt safe wedged between Crystal and a woman with blackened teeth and bleached, straw-textured hair whom I had seen before selling sex around Clapham Common.

The conversation turned to scams, successful or otherwise.

'What works for me is going into the smaller places to nick stuff where the security camera doesn't cover all the shelves all the time. If you're quick you can be in and out before the camera has swivelled your way,' laughed one man with bony wrists and a downy half-centimetre of ginger hair. Men cursed with that fiery shade of hair often seem to try and crop it out of existence.

'No, man, the best jobs are those little corner shops. Even if they see you nicking stuff they're too scared to do anything about it and by the time they've called the police you can be miles away.'

The discussion about the relative merits of different illicit income-generation schemes continued. Some voices were strident, others were dreamy. I sat bolt upright and said nothing. Despite the confidence-boosting effects of the crack I still felt very apprehensive about actually, finally, sitting inside a crack house. I wondered if there were any surprises still awaiting me, like a malevolent rabbit suddenly bounding out of a magician's hat. I tried to relax and rested my head against the back of the sofa. I closed my eyes and inhaled the odour of feet that had been in shoes and socks for too long and baked bicarbonate of soda. As I was to discover, every crack house smelt the same. While crack houses do a roaring trade every day and night of the year, the customers, many of whom would be described by Social Services as 'vulnerably housed', stayed in the crack houses to smoke during the cold winter months, sometimes huddled together with others for warmth. During the summer, people had their own secluded spots to go to in shady corners of parks or draughty squats that were uninhabitable when it got too cold.

Crystal appeared to be in her element *chez* Pete. She found the scam tips uproariously funny and her huge blue eyes opened even wider each time one of the men shared some new knowledge with us. People were gushingly nice to me.

'Oh, you're called Rhea, what a beautiful name. You're working, are you? Oh, a hairdresser – that's fantastic, must be so interesting. Good tips, I expect. Hope you don't go around sniffing the hairspray when the manager's back is turned, ha ha.' I truly believed they were interested in me because I was such an appealing human being. I underestimated the extent of manipulation of the average crack addict. They flattered me because I was working, because unlike them I looked not only clean but relatively well dressed and so they assumed I had money, more money than they had, at least, and money which, perhaps, if enough compliments came my way, I could be prevailed upon to share with them when it came to buying the next round.

I began to slot into life at Pete's crack house. Gradually I began smoking more and more crack, sometimes took days off work, although I managed not to get fired, and began to blend in much better with the other people around me.

After a couple of months, Bob, the dealer in the kitchen, disappeared. He was a monosyllabic Jamaican man with shoulder-length dreadlocks whom I never heard use any parts of his vocabulary other than 'How much ya need now?' or 'Got no change today', so that anyone lucky enough to be in possession of a £20 note rather than a £10 would be persuaded to part with it. Some dealers did special offers for those who bought brown (heroin) and white (crack) but he didn't seem to have that supermarket mentality and insisted on charging full price for what he said was 'good-quality stuff'.

When Bob left without explanation he sub-contracted the sale of his merchandise to a couple of boys who couldn't have been more than fifteen or sixteen.

'I'm glad he's gone,' I said to Crystal. 'With these two boys not much older than Paul here I'm sure we'll be able to wheedle a little bit of extra crack out of them. I bet they won't be as tough as Bob was on us.'

I couldn't have been more wrong. On the second day at the helm both of them grabbed me and dragged me into the bathroom and one pulled out a short, shiny knife and held it against my throat. The boys tried to pull my jeans down. I screamed and a man I'd never seen before came running. Nobody else moved.

'Oi, what the fuck do you think you're doing? Move from her. Holding the house doesn't mean you run the world, you know.'

The boys let go of me, and with a surly stare at my saviour, sauntered off back into the kitchen.

'Come into the bedroom where it's quiet and I'll sit with you for a while,' he said. I was suspicious but he seemed genuine. We sat more or less in silence for a couple of hours. I offered him some crack but he refused it and he made no sexual advances towards me.

'I don't want anything from you,' he kept saying.

The silence was companionable and even the battered bed stripped of sheets and the torn curtains began to look quite appealing. The brazen attack on me by the two young dealers had not only terrified me but made me despair of human nature. Sitting peacefully with this stranger, whom incidentally I never saw again, restored my faith in human beings.

As I gained in confidence I started to try out different crack houses, sometimes accompanied by Crystal, sometimes boldly going into these places alone. But always my visits had to fit around my childcare commitments. A network of friends and babysitters made sure they were cared for when I was absent and I in turn helped them out with caring for their children. As I ventured inside more and more crack houses I began to get a sense of who the typical users were – people living on local estates with dull or unhappy lives. One reason why people give up crack once they've fallen into the depths with it is because they've got something good in their lives that helps them to pull themselves out of the abyss. For many of the people whom I saw over and over again there wasn't actually anything better than crack in their lives and so they continued to smoke.

Not everyone fitted the stereotype of estate dweller with few prospects. One beautiful young woman, whose accent sounded to me exactly like the Queen's, began, timidly at first, to frequent crack houses. She had expensively highlighted shoulder-length blonde hair and designer clothes. By the time I met her I was a very experienced visitor to crack houses. With a group of other people, I offered to score her some crack to protect her from the volatility of the crack house she was about to enter.

'The dealer in that house is quite heavy,' I warned her.

'Would you like me to go and score for you? I'll meet you back here on the edge of the estate in fifteen minutes.'

Gratefully she pressed £100 into my hands. To my eternal shame I headed straight for another crack house and spent her money on drugs for myself and the group of people I was with. I occasionally see her selling sex on the streets of south London. Her looks are beginning to go and she's lost a couple of teeth. Crack is a great leveller.

14. A TEMPORARY DEATH

Birthdays were always big events for Paul and Keira. They were both born in May and I usually had one big party for them, buying large amounts of food and treats and inviting their friends, my friends and members of the family. They were always happy, lively occasions with the children MCing into polystyrene cups and lots of music and dancing. I remember my mother holding a birthday party for me when I was four years old and inviting lots of people from my nursery school. Only two turned up and I burned with shame. I was determined that Paul and Keira's parties would have people spilling out of every room.

'This is your special day,' I always told them both. 'It's the day when you're the most important person in the world and everything is happening just for you.' I saved up for months to order them branded trainers from catalogues, to make sure that there were plates of sandwiches and crisps and fairy cakes piled high on the table and most of all that there was a big, colourfully iced birthday cake as the centrepiece.

Every mother has a plan for her children. I wanted mine to know that they were at the centre of my universe and

I wanted them to feel loved every second of their lives. But sadly events got in the way.

When Paul was eleven and Keira was four I was sliding inexorably towards the world of chaos and crack. I always made sure that there was food in the fridge and that they got to school on time but I felt rudderless as I struggled through with them. Whenever I could get a babysitter I went to my local pub, the Mason's Arms, where there were plenty of people buying and selling drugs. I sold ecstasy pills to fund my crack habit. The bouncers watched out for me and I became part of an all-male crew of dealers in the pub. I loved being part of this charmed circle of hard men whom everybody buzzed towards. I was tough and refused to tolerate hard luck stories from impoverished addicts. The pub dealing was a good apprenticeship for what was to come.

I experimented with ketamine, an increasingly popular club drug. It was a terrifying experience. I lost all use of my legs and temporarily went blind. I was hallucinating within hallucinations – a process known as disappearing into a K-hole. I couldn't understand what people saw in the drug and never touched it again. Crack was a different story, though. All I wanted to do night and day was to smoke crack. Crack cradles you in its fumes, suspends you from the usual constraints of time and space. With crack, for the few minutes that its effects lasted, I wasn't a failure, I had no shortcomings and it held all my problems away on the other side of the see-through sphere. Everything looked perfectly straightforward and soluble. Only things didn't look that way when the chemical euphoria faded. They looked more intractable than ever and the only way out was more crack, more oblivion and more removal from reality.

One of the crack users I met at the Mason's Arms was a rather vicious man who was attached to a smelly colostomy bag. In the way that some people do in the world of Class A drugs, he insinuated himself into my home and once over the threshold was impossible to remove. He sat in my bedroom smoking crack all day long. I was terrified of calling the police in case they discovered that I too was smoking crack and took my children away.

I continued to make futile attempts to remove him.

'Please, Pete, having you here is such a bad thing for the children. For their sake if not for mine, please get out.'

'Shan't,' he said petulantly. 'What yer going to do, call the cops on me? They'll probably take you away before they touch me. You're not really a fit mother, are you, stuffing crack into your lungs morning, noon and night?'

I knew he was right and cowered, defeated in my own home, gritting my teeth against my loathed guest. Eventually I appealed to Darren to try and get him out. It was the first time I'd asked for his help since we'd broken up and I had to swallow a lot of pride to do it but there simply didn't seem to be any alternative. I failed to mention that both of us were smoking crack.

Darren was supportive and agreed to come to my house to ask Pete to leave. When he arrived, Pete was sitting on my bed smoking crack. The game was up. Darren looked from me to Pete and then back to me, shaking his head slowly.

'You better scarper this minute, mate, or you'll be in bigger trouble than you've ever known.'

Pete took one look at Darren, who was far taller and broader than him, swept his drugs paraphernalia into a Tesco carrier bag and sprinted out of the front door.

The relief I felt at seeing Pete leave was almost entirely eclipsed by my feelings of shame and humiliation at being caught red-handed with a crack smoker in my house.

Darren said little but when he did speak, his words were deadly.

'I'll have to take the kids, Rhea,' he said. 'Just for a couple of weeks until you sort yourself out.'

I stood rooted to the spot, tears splashing onto the wooden floorboards of the kitchen. I watched as he helped Paul and Keira put some clothes and favourite toys into a bag and ushered them out of the house.

'Mummy's not very well but you'll be back as soon as she's better,' Darren said, trying to sound soothing. Paul remained tight-lipped and expressionless; Keira cried even more than I did.

'I promise I'll collect you soon,' I said, my voice jumping with sobs. 'Don't forget I love you both very much. You're my life.'

I felt as if I had no insides left. I wasn't a real mother, I was a fraud. All the things I had strived for for my children were worthless because ultimately I had failed to protect them against the big bad world. As I became increasingly unable to cope with the demands of motherhood and maintain a grip on 'normal' existence I had taken to self-harming to release emotional pain and stress. The act of slashing my forearms worked remarkably well at dispersing tension and making me feel peaceful.

When the front door slammed with me on one side of it and Darren and the children moving further and further away from me on the other side I felt as if the door was my coffin lid, banging shut, trapping me inside my final resting place forever. I'd died in one world and my children were dead to me in another. My life was over and there was no way back up to the surface of the earth. I got a razor blade out of the bathroom cupboard and started slashing randomly at my forearms. But I found almost no relief this time. I jumped in my car and drove to Crystal's house. I hadn't seen her for months but she was the first person I thought of to share my despair with. I needed someone who would encourage me to use even more drugs than I was planning to use, someone who wouldn't make me feel guilty about using. I was still blinded by tears when I arrived at her house. She was making a half-hearted attempt at doing the washing up.

'Oh, Crystal, I'm so glad you're home. I've lost my children, I've lost everything, there's nothing left and no point in going on,' I said.

I poured out everything to her. She sat listening carefully, put a sympathetic arm around my shoulders and listened until I was all talked out. Then she carefully wiped away my tears with a crumpled tissue and said, 'Let's go and score.'

She sounded motherly, as if she were prescribing a nice cup of tea or perhaps a comforting bowl of chicken soup. We lost ourselves in crack for a few hours until it was time to collect her daughter Anya from school.

As promised I picked my children up from Stella, Darren's mother, a couple of weeks later. She greeted me with her warm, throaty laugh. Her big house was always full of children and grandchildren. Food was always either being prepared, eaten or cleared away and I knew that at least here Paul and Keira would be safe from harm.

When I collected them I felt no better about my mothering skills than I did when Darren took them away from me. I was gripped with fear at my uselessness as a parent. I was scared to engage with them, to touch them even, in case I contaminated them with my lousy parenting. They looked at me puzzled as I panicked and quivered. Voices in my head kept taunting me with the words: 'You're a useless mother, you never should have had children. How could you possibly think you could cope with this parenting lark? Give them up, give them up; they'll be better off without you.'

In the end, beaten, with nobody to turn to, I delivered them back to Darren's mother's house. I promised I'd be back to collect them soon but the weeks slipped into months. During this period of utter desolation I took several paracetamol overdoses. I hoarded forty or fifty pills at a time and then swallowed them all in the space of a few minutes. I felt that I'd failed as a mother and that if I couldn't even look after the two innocent children whom I'd taken a decision to bring into the world there was no point in me continuing to be alive. I decided that they'd be better off without me, that Darren's mother would love them and treat them as her own, as would my own mother. I didn't take the overdoses as a cry for help, I took them because I wanted to die and had lost all hope for myself. I thought that my family would actually be better off without my troublesome, wayward presence in the world. But none of the overdoses killed me nor did they seem to do any significant damage to my vital organs. Generally I felt woozy and disoriented when I took the pills but I didn't slip into a coma and they didn't remove my woes. I began to wonder if survival was my destiny, if, like rats or grey squirrels, I would be able to constantly evolve, to triumph over my genes.

Soon after I'd taken one pile of pills my mother called me. She could hear that I sounded very unwell, dropped everything and drove from Bristol to London to be with me. 'Oh my God, Rhea, what have you done to yourself?' she said, tears springing into her eyes when she saw me. I could only groan in reply, not because I was unable to speak but because there was nothing I could bear to say.

She drove me down to the local hospital where I was checked over and kept in overnight for observation. The doctors noticed the long, white scars on my arms and the fresher wounds where I'd cut myself a few days before and became even more worried than they had been initially about me.

There was discussion about referring me to a psychiatric hospital as an inpatient. The thought of that happening made me feel even worse. I decided I had to start acting and tried to remember how I'd feigned sincerity when I'd worked as a hostess in Soho.

'I don't think there's any need for that,' I said. 'Taking this overdose has really brought me to my senses. I realise now that the last thing I want to do is die. I know I need help but I don't think being in a psychiatric hospital will do anything to aid my recovery.'

The doctor looked at me doubtfully but then agreed to refer me for a series of outpatient appointments.

'Thank you doctor. I promise I'll keep the appointments. This overdose has been a real wake-up call for me.'

I was discharged the following day with a referral letter. The overdose had been a wake-up call of sorts. I didn't try to end my life again but decided instead that I would stick to crack to numb my pain. I urged my worried mother to go back to Bristol and promised her I'd call her regularly. I never made it to my outpatient appointments.

The children seemed to be reasonably settled with Stella. Seeing them search my face with their trusting, bewildered eyes when I went round to visit them was too much for me. I fled back to Crystal's house and became a fugitive. Miraculously, the voices stopped.

15. DEPUTY CEO

Without my children to keep me in touch with the real world I tumbled further and further down. I felt as if I was trapped in a dizzying series of somersaults. I became more and more giddy but couldn't find a way to stop spinning lower and lower. I let my hairdressing job go. I had been motivated to keep turning up for work in order to support my children but now they were gone I didn't have the energy to pretend I didn't have a crack habit while I was at work. I handed in my notice and began to sell sex in a systematic way on the streets of south London. I was very thin, barely a size eight, and in my mini skirt and fishnet tights with my cropped hair dyed peroxide blonde I managed to attract enough punters to keep my habit going. I never once baulked at the work although I hated it. Feeling numb and smoking enough crack to keep that feeling going were all that mattered. Punters were a means to an end and for that I tolerated them. Other women I knew from crack houses told me the best and busiest streets to stand on and although there was competition between us there was also camaraderie. We all had sympathy for each other's desperate plight and saw ourselves reflected in the desperate eyes of the other women we gazed at. I and the other women sometimes brought punters who were partial to the little white rocks back to one of the crack houses to have sex with them. This pleased the house dealers no end because it was extra business for them. If a man was having sex he was likely to spend more money on crack than he otherwise would to heighten the experience. It was while I was to-ing and fro-ing between street and crack house, often with a man on my arm, that I met DP.

I didn't become Angel until I met him. He was the crack dealer I got to know best of all. I had a tattoo on my back which said 'Angel'. It was supposed to be an ironic reference to the life I was leading. I often wore low-cut, strappy tops to attract punters so the tattoo was on display for everyone to see. The first time I met DP and we got chatting, I sensed that I was about to enter a new and more dangerous phase of my life. Perhaps if I was still looking after my children I would have turned my back on what was eventually proposed to me. But without Paul and Keira I couldn't think of a good enough reason to say no.

Previously I had not got into conversations with dealers. I had simply given my order and handed over my money. In the course of many of these transactions the dealers either nodded or shrugged but didn't open their mouths. DP was different, though. He appeared to be interested in me beyond the £10 note clutched in my hand. The thrilling, gangster-filled world he inhabited drew me towards him. I decided that only more and more extreme experiences could numb my sense of loss. Consorting with hard-faced gangsters with sawn-off shotguns concealed inside their long coats fitted the bill. And in order to persuade myself further I reasoned that ingratiating myself with DP would lead to free handouts of crack. I did my best to nurture his interest. The crack house was quiet when we first started chatting and he seemed in no hurry to end the conversation once I'd paid him for my crack.

'What's your name?' he asked, cocking his head attentively on one side.

I was apprehensive about giving my real name. I tried to look coy while frantically racking my brains for a false name to give him.

'What's that you've got written on your back?' He twisted his head round to look. 'Angel! So is that your name?'

Angel sounded perfect.

'Yes, that'll do,' I said, smiling broadly. A new name was a chance to reinvent myself as a beautiful, shining person.

I often thought that DP had chosen the wrong career path. He was tall, slim and toned and took his health very seriously. All of the Jamaican crack dealers were loosely referred to as Yardies although few of them were, in the strictest sense of the word. He often sat reflecting quietly while all around him was boisterous chaos. Paranoid crack users sometimes found his silence terrifying. I imagined him with a notepad propped against his knees, scribbling lines of poetry about God, the world and the importance of respecting the body. Alternatively I think he would have done well as a personal trainer, exhorting plump, burger-eating youngsters to turn their backs on junk food and forcing them to complete just one more circuit at the gym.

He would have been truly affronted if anyone had offered him a rock of crack to smoke. Even those who presumed to offer him a cigarette or something alcoholic were given short shrift. DP described his body as a 'shrine' and never saw any irony in providing others with the means to destroy theirs.

'You gotta protect ya body, Angel. It's de only one dat de Good Lord gave ya.'

DP only ever drank water, herbal teas and freshly squeezed vegetable juices, which he bought from West Indian shops. He religiously did at least 100 press-ups and

100 sit-ups every day and I imagined that if his skin was removed to expose his muscles they'd be as polished and gleaming as his teeth. As he worked out, his shoulder-length dreadlocks, tied up neatly, swished from one side of his neck to the other.

'Look at all dose smackheads with da terrible teeth,' he used to tut-tut to me. He religiously flossed his strong white teeth every morning and evening and banned sugary products from passing his lips.

DP was fond of making pronouncements, most of them, it seemed, to me. He'd decided to make me his protégée and wanted to impart all of his wisdom to this junk-eating, crack-smoking young woman with no interest in exercise.

'Sugar is de enemy, Angel, and that's an important lesson in life,' he often said.

I had never been as strategic about anything as I was about gaining DP's trust and admiration. When I first met him he had recruited a dealer to sell drugs in his crack house but he slumbered on the job far too often. The problem of sleep deprivation was one that afflicted all dealers. If you want to get ahead in the world of selling Class A drugs you have to permit yourself about as much sleep as anorexics permit themselves food. The less you sleep and the more you're on the end of the phone or servicing the crack house, the more money you'll earn and the more your reputation will grow as a dealer the desperate can count on in their hour of need.

'I'm not happy about the number of times I've caught Tom sleeping on the job,' grumbled DP. I was keen to stoke up the fire of DP's discontent in the hope that Tom's loss could be my gain.

'I know what you mean, DP,' I said, trying to make my voice sound silken soothing. 'Customers have been complaining that Tom hasn't been doing his job properly. And I know people have taken advantage of him a few times and robbed him.'

DP nodded grimly. 'We'll have to do something about that.'

This went on for several months. I observed, became a faithful, patient disciple and behaved well in DP's presence. I ingratiated myself with him by networking at the Mason's Arms pub, selecting the more trustworthy lovers of crack for invitation to DP's crack house. My referrals swelled DP's business considerably. As I helped DP a plan was forming in my mind. I had very rarely seen a woman selling crack outside a crack house and never inside one, but I wanted DP to let me sell drugs for him in his crack house. There were many strands of motivation that wove in and out of each other. I wanted to be as strong and tough as the male crack dealers I knew; I wanted to be their equal rather than a subservient woman, selling her body for rocks (I and the other women who did this were referred to rather unflatteringly as crack whores). I retained the residue of weakness I had felt when I had been beaten by Leroy and Billy and I felt that taking on a role where I had total power over a group of customers would banish that frailty in me.

I had never moved very far from the crack house at the bottom of the supply ladder and at last one evening my teacher DP decided he was going to trust me to place my feet on the first rung. He had already allowed me to drive his car around on domestic errands. Like all self-respecting crack dealers, DP drove a Mercedes. It was a slightly battered silver one but that only served to enhance his credibility – he saw himself as an 'old money' dealer rather than the flashy bling-style vendor who had literally got rich overnight. DP prided himself on growing his drugs business at a slower and more sustainable rate than some of his rivals. I was a good driver and I basked behind the wheel as DP's chosen sidekick. Being selected made me feel important and, in a strictly business sense, adored. DP also provided a home delivery service for those of his customers whose delicate sensibilities made the idea of stepping over the threshold of a crack house rather distasteful. This refined group felt more comfortable smoking themselves silly in the privacy of their own homes. DP took me along with him when he made his deliveries. Those moments when we knocked on doors, particularly the doors of people I knew, I swelled with pride. I was the chosen one. I felt I had achieved. Sometimes DP asked me to take his car and make deliveries alone.

Allowing me to drive his car was part of the grooming process. Everything started to fall into place – the increasing responsibility DP was placing on my shoulders and then the sacking of Tom, the sleepy dealer. After weeks of consideration, DP made his decision.

'I'm going to have to let you go, Tom. Your working performance just ain't happening, is it?' said DP, shaking his head and pretending to look sad. There was not much Tom could do apart from skulk out of the door, never to be seen again. He no doubt feared DP might raise his fist to him if he tried to argue. And when you work in a crack house you don't really have much recourse to employment rights. I imagine that Tom found the nearest bed to collapse on to and slept for a very, very long time.

'I could sit in the house and sell for you a few days a week if you like,' I offered casually. DP raised his eyebrows.

'Do you think you could manage that, Angel?'

I'd visited many crack houses over the years but I've never seen a woman enthroned in the dealer's chair. I nodded, trying not to look too excited.

'Well, I would like to train you up to take over from Tom,' said DP thoughtfully.

'I know it's not usually a job for a woman but I think I'd be very efficient at it,' I said, simpering, in the hope that he would praise my innate dealer talents. He did.

'I know that, I know that. You're good, you're smart and you don't stand for no rubbish. Look, I'll show you how I want my tings to be run.'

He took out a small pair of black, digital scales and a big lump of crack that nestled comfortably in the palm of his hand. Strong sunlight streamed through the window making the crack glint like a big empty eye without the eyeball. My eyes started to water and my heart started to pound at the sight of so much crack.

'Now, cut it carefully, making as few crumbs as possible, otherwise you'll be wasting all ma profit, and wrap it like so.' Although I had unwrapped thousands of rocks, I had never wrapped the stuff up. I tried to place my brain in reverse and managed to do a dealer wrap perfectly after a couple of tries.

'Good, Angel, good. You're a quick learner. That's why I singled you out to assist me. Now, what's my golden rule?'

'No credit, DP, no matter whether your granny's just dropped dead, you were robbed on the way to the crack house, you're about to come into some money and will pay up tomorrow. Never believe a crackhead's excuse. Whatever line they try on, the answer is always a loud, clear no.'

'Excellent, Angel, that's the right answer. Make sure you stick to that with da customers and then you and me, we'll be OK.' He touched my cheek softly with his knuckles. It was his way of praising me. I unfolded myself into DP's approval. Dealing drugs was one of the few things I'd ever received praise for in my life. I couldn't believe that I was about to enter this bastion of male power. I didn't feel strong inside myself but having a huge lump of crack as an accessory transformed the sense of my own strength and importance. This was the first time I could remember engineering a situation to my own advantage instead of simply waiting for an out-of-control train to hit me.

DP always carried a gun although he usually concealed it. I didn't know the difference between one gun and another. DP's gun was very small, almost like a toy one, but the hard, silvery glint of it didn't look remotely fake. I had never seen DP use it but every now and again he took it out of its resting place in an inside pocket in his leather jacket, and fingered it thoughtfully before returning it to the pocket. People sometimes saw him doing this and no one ever argued with him. He offered me a gun to protect myself. I was terrified of having such a thing anywhere near me but he was persuasive. I placed it in my handbag, trembling. While the prospect of firing a gun and the consequences of doing so terrified me, the gangster allure of being around men with guns was stronger than magnets for me. I was still at that childlike point in my life where I didn't process consequences. All I was capable of doing was involving myself in the pleasures and pains of the very immediate present.

Despite his gun, DP was much gentler than some of the crack dealers I came across in other houses. Once I had been in a crack house run by a particularly malevolent, violent dealer called Tag. Whenever the house dealer he'd appointed, Bryn, fell asleep, Tag used to creep up behind him and punch him awake with a blow to the back of the neck. A desperate, emaciated prostitute called Kay had found a stray kitten whining by the large dustbins on the estate where the crack house was. She picked it up and cuddled it. The kitten stared soulfully into her eyes. She stared back. It was love at first sight. She took the kitten up to the crack house, announced to everyone that a formal adoption process had taken place and tried to coax the kitten into drinking some milk. She placed him on the floor so that he could sip milk from a chipped plate she'd found in the kitchen.

'Whatever you do don't open the front door or he'll run away,' she said plaintively to the small group who had assembled in the hallway to coo over him.

While everyone admired the kitten, Tag quietly opened the front door. The kitten started at the sound and darted out.

'You fucking bastard, how could you do that?' wailed Kay, turning on Tag. 'That kitten was my little bit of something to love and you took it away from me. You opened that door on purpose.'

Tag looked at her for a few seconds then, enraged at her humiliation of him in front of others, picked up a piece of wood and started beating her viciously around the head. Everyone ducked as he kept on swinging the wood at her head and her body. By the time his anger was spent she was drenched in blood. She staggered out of the crack house screaming. Her injuries took many months to heal.

DP, who was something of a perfectionist, left me with forty rocks neatly wrapped, which I placed in a paper cup. The drill was that if the police raided, everyone moved as far away from the paper cup as possible so that the police could not prove who had been dealing. The police knew about DP and were very keen to catch him red-handed. One time they raided the crack house, found no drugs but started hunting for DP.

'Where's the big man, then?' said one of the officers. 'We know he was here about twenty minutes ago.' As usual DP had evaded capture. Although his and the police's paths almost crossed almost all the time, it was as if he was wrapped in some kind of anti-police cling-film which protected him from arrest. No matter how hard they tried they never managed to accost him with either lumps of crack or wads of cash on him. But I think that that level of perpetual alertness took its toll. Despite his wholesome diet and healthy habits, the pressure to keep the drugs and money moving all the time and the fear of a police officer's hand clamping itself to his shoulder as he glided noiselessly down a dark alley made him apprehensive.

The crack house I was presiding over was a pretty convivial one. The living conditions, fixtures and furnishings inside a crack house were largely dependent on how long ago real people had led normal lives in the place.

This flat, on the top floor of a council block, had belonged to the mother of the current tenant, Jimmy. While his mother was alive he was an occasional dabbler but when she died grief transformed him from a recreational user to a hopeless addict. She had died six months previously and he agreed to hand the flat over to DP in exchange for free drugs. He was an only child and he and his mother had been very close. The crack house community became like a substitute family for him. The signs of his mother's presence were still strong – lots of family photographs on the wall, an array of hideous china ornaments and a comfortable brown three-piece suite. Occasionally Jimmy would say dolefully, 'I can't believe I'm smoking crack in a dead woman's house.' The TV still worked and sometimes we listened to music on pirate radio stations. *Coronation Street* and *EastEnders* were crack house favourites. We gazed at the Mitchell brothers or Ken Barlow while we drooled over our pipes.

One of the reasons why the crack house had survived in a reasonable state for so long was because DP was very selective about the people he allowed through the door. There was an intercom on the ground floor and only known regulars were buzzed upstairs. Very occasionally DP would sell drugs on the street and if he decided that the buyer was reliable he would signpost them towards his crack house. DP's caution paid off. We only got raided once by the police while I was there. It was a moment of unusual serendipity. It was rare that there was a crack drought on but on this day there was one. DP couldn't get hold of the drug and we were all sitting in the house with nothing more incriminating than a few crack pipes for the police to stumble upon. This obviously wasn't an intelligence-led operation. Raiding a crack house during a crack drought is not the way for officers to meet their monthly crime-busting targets.

I sat at one end of the three-piece suite doling out crack to the unkempt, skinny customers who formed an orderly queue, holding £10 notes in their outstretched palms. Weirdly it reminded me of the scene in the film *Oliver Twist* when the ragged boys queue up for gruel.

As the usual stories of hardship and appeals for credit spilled from them, I folded my arms and pursed my lips.

'You know there's no credit in DP's crack house,' I said with less sympathy than a dead goldfish, despite my own recent experiences of begging for credit in the same way as they now were. I felt arrogant. I no longer inhabited their world. In the very recent past I had ingratiated myself with dealers in the hope that they would donate me the crumbs that dropped on to the table when the crack was cut up. Now it was my turn to play God. I felt like Queen Victoria, drawing an invisible line in the sand between the deserving and the undeserving junkies.

I stored the money in my shoe and whenever I had reached around £100 I called DP, who came to relieve me of it. Keeping the money and the drugs constantly on the move is key to success for any dealer. Being caught with a significant quantity of either was far too risky. Small quantities of drugs could be stored in the mouth or the nether regions and cash could be laundered by a variety of shady characters who ran down-at-heel bureaux de change or garages with money-lending businesses on the side. DP used to call into the crack house first thing in the morning, swigging from a large carton of carrot juice, checking that the number of rocks sold and amount of money handed over for them tallied exactly. He was meticulous and knew exactly how much money he expected me to hand over. I gave him a pile of £10 notes from crack sold in the early hours of the morning. He counted them in silence and then nodded to me. 'It's all there. Well done, Angel. I know my instinct about you is right.'

I adored being in charge. I felt iconic as I sat on the sofa coolly appraising the people who lined up for their fix. From the age of thirteen I had been rebelling against a world I neither liked nor fitted into. Now I felt I had reached the pinnacle of that rebellion. There was no greater act of dissent than selling crack in a crack house. I wondered if I was the first female crack dealer to ever hold court in a crack house. I was a pioneer, a warrior of sorts, like Boudica. But I wasn't fighting for any sort of cause. My rebellion was an empty one which I began not because something mattered terribly to me but because nothing mattered at all. The male customers seemed to love my Marilyn Monroe shade of blonde locks and the revealing strappy tops that I wore whatever the weather. My image dovetailed neatly with the rest of their fantasies about crack and sex.

Before DP took over Jimmy's mother's flat, he had run another crack house which I visited once. It couldn't have been more different. It was like walking into Beirut in the middle of the war: filthy, smelly and anarchic. The state of crack houses was often dependent on where they were. Those in more visible, main road locations were far busier and therefore got wrecked more quickly by customers. They also had a shorter lifespan as they were more likely to get raided. Dealers had to make a commercial decision about whether they preferred to run a more sustainable crack house slightly off the beaten track with a slower turnover or a crash-and-burn one where large profits could be made in a short time before the place was closed down by police. When DP pondered the relative merits of longevity and a fast buck, he chose the former. It turned out to be a shrewd decision because apart from the one occasion when the police raided during the crack drought they left us alone.

Many crack houses are unspeakably filthy. Some have no running water, which means no working toilets, no electricity and no heating, but I was determined to keep Jimmy's mother's flat looking presentable for as long as possible, partly in memory of her and partly because the customers really appreciated having a decent living room to sit in to smoke their crack. I prided myself on the cleanliness and good order of the crack house being a unique selling point in a jungle of smelly, stripped flats with no water or heating and not even a nod towards civilised living. There was usually at least an hour or two during the day when trade was quiet. Sometimes I snatched sleep then but at other times, powered by crack adrenalin, I scrubbed the kitchen sink, mopped the floor and poured copious amounts of economy bleach down the toilet. Sometimes when things were quiet I popped down to the supermarket, bought a loaf of bread and a box of eggs and cooked whoever was in the flat eggs on toast.

'This is the nicest, cleanest, most comfortable crack house I've ever been into,' declared one customer, a pasty-faced white man with light brown dreadlocks. The more people liked the crack house, the longer they stayed, the more money they spent and the happier DP was. I decided that if crack houses ever got involved with the kind of contests that the straight business world enjoyed, I would be very likely to win employee of the year.

16. PROMOTION

In the illegal world of selling and using drugs, the crack house is fairly near the bottom of an elaborate system of pyramid selling. The men – and I do believe it is men rather than women, although I never met any of them – close to the top receive cocaine and heroin in tens of kilos when it arrives in the UK by boat or plane. Usually they will sell the drugs on in kilos and then the drugs cascade downwards through a series of intermediaries in little stops and starts like an electronic waterfall until they reach the panting addicts waiting to catch the drops at the bottom. By the time it reaches those begging on the ground, who are invariably poverty-stricken, the profits have accumulated handsomely for the various vendors. The dealers who run the crack houses are often more ruthless than the street dealers. The former are hard-headed businessmen while the latter are just selling drugs to try and get by. I don't think the street dealers see a huge amount of profit from their drugs but the dealers in the crack houses benefit from the prostitutes who bring lots of crack-smoking customers back with them. Those girls work very hard for their little white rocks while the house dealer seems to have relatively little to do in comparison apart from stroke his gun, discipline the rowdy and watch the money roll in.

I often wondered how the drug scene would change if everyone could grow their own opium poppies and coca plants on scrubby bits of land beside their inner-city tower blocks or in their suburban back gardens.

Of course the people at the top, middle and bottom of the supply chain would more or less be out of a job, crime rates would plummet and lawyers, judges and prison and probation officers would, like the dealers and traffickers, be largely redundant.

If the drugs were as easily available as rain falling out of the sky, would people use them differently, stripped of the current ritual of procuring money for a fix, meeting up with the dealer or stepping through the reinforced front door of a crack house followed by the very precise routine of preparing the drugs for smoking or injection? Perhaps they'd lose interest and find another diversion or perhaps their habits would escalate and many would be even more lost than they are under current arrangements.

The process of preparing drugs for smoking or injecting is not something that the uninitiated would ever manage without a careful teacher at their side. Even a first-year pharmacy student would require guidance from an addict expert in these matters. Crack addicts who think they are concealing their habit well are often given away by the traces of soot inside their nails as well as the ripped, blackened skin on their fingertips from battering a piece of gauze into submission in the crack pipe. To smoke crack, both the pipe and the drug have to be prepared. Miniature spirits bottles make the best crack pipes. A rock of crack has to be melted on to a piece of gauze – then to smoke the drug the lighter needs to be flicked on and off and the fumes inhaled. If too constant a heat is applied, the neck of the bottle will crack, so, as with the other parts of this rather convoluted process, a combination of skill and experience is required.

People refer to smoking crack as a 'steam', perhaps because the sensation the drug produces is as intense as having steam come out of your head. The debris left in a pipe after a smoking session is known as the recycle. When several smoking sessions' worth have accumulated, it can be resmoked for a particularly potent hit. For that reason and the fact that it is a bit of a performance converting a spirit bottle into a crack pipe, people guard their smoking equipment ferociously. As with the preparation of heroin for injecting, there is an enormous amount of ritual associated with smoking crack, and the sense of anticipation associated with the preparation of the drugs provides almost as big a buzz as the chemicals themselves.

Smoking crack affects people in different ways. It gave me a curiously bloated feeling. If I was sitting in a crack house I felt the need to undo my trousers, as if I had just consumed an enormous meal. If I was somewhere more private I would put on shorts and a strappy top so that I wouldn't feel constricted. Interruptions during a smoking session were very unwelcome. There's a lot of greed associated with crack and any attempts at conversation by others spoiled the purity of the high. Like my clothes, life felt as if it was stifling me but crack changed that. It was a hoovering out of the mind; it made me feel totally free and happy, unfettered by any of the usual human considerations. I could think clearly about things that seemed muddled. But of course this clarity was a mirage. When the effects wore off my problems were as insoluble and as complex as they were before.

If I had the money I could spend £400 in a thirty-six-hour smoking binge, smoking so much crack that I felt very nauseous. It horrifies me now to think of burning so much money but at the time it all seemed perfectly rational and reasonable.

Before I began injecting heroin alongside crack, I very much looked down on injectors. In the drug-taking hierarchy they were at the bottom. I regarded them as dirty, smelly, weak-willed creatures who couldn't hold things together. They developed revolting, weeping blood- and pus-filled abscesses on parts of their bodies where they injected over and over again. Although I recoiled from heroin I experienced that familiar pull towards it, a fascination with something that was dangerous and repugnant.

Crack was sold in elaborately wrapped pieces of clear clingfilm; heroin was first wrapped in pieces of turquoise polythene carrier bags, the kinds used by corner shops. On top of the turquoise polythene, clingfilm was placed. It always amazed me how rigidly all the dealers stuck to the turquoise and clear film code for the two drugs they sold – like the products sold in shops in the former Soviet Union when the Cold War was at its height.

'Blue for brown and white for white,' said DP to me soon after we first met. 'Obvious, innit.'

Opening the wrap of heroin involved great care and attention to detail. If it was done carelessly the valuable drug would be spilt. I watched addicts steadily, lovingly open their precious packages. They had the same express-ions of deep concentration on their faces as experts trying to safely detonate a bomb before it could blow up a shopping centre. They tipped the brown powder on to the spoon so that none of it was wasted. Some held the syringe in their mouths while preparing a vein for injection with a tourniquet. I observed carefully and made a detailed mental note of what was going on.

DP didn't have much patience with crack users but he had even less with heroin users and wouldn't tolerate them openly injecting in his crack house in case some harm befell them (like death) which would rebound catastrophically on him. He encouraged me to clamp down on injectors and was so pleased with my policing abilities that he decided to give me more responsibility.

'Angel, I can't meet ma man tonight to restock,' said DP one afternoon when supplies were running low. 'I trust you, truly I do. If I give you ma money and ma motor could you carry out the transaction for me?'

In the world of the crack house I was a confident queen bee. When I cut up the crack into tiny £10 rocks my hand remained steady. When I dealt with customers I considered myself to be firm but fair and when it came to maintaining some sort of order I was pretty efficient. But going out of that strangely safe, closeted world to consort with a dealer further up the supply chain than DP was terrifying. I knew how to hide the stash of crack if police raided the crack house but if I was caught red-handed in a car by the police I would be entirely helpless. Penalties for dealing substantial quantities of drugs were harsh and I didn't particularly fancy spending several years in jail. In my mind the madness of my crack life was a temporary interlude before I reclaimed my beloved children and acquired the dream house in suburbia that I'd been denied as a child.

But I didn't want to disappoint DP and his belief in my capacity to achieve as a crucial link in the chain of command, so I gulped and nodded my head.

'OK, DP, it'll be good for me to learn the business a bit more.'

He nodded and allowed himself a small, enigmatic smile.

'I'll give you my phone and dis guy will call you on it before you do da business with him. Here's ma car keys and here's ma phone. I've told Dex that you'll meet him in Broughton Road, that little side street off Park Road, at 2 a.m. He'll come into the car and you'll need to switch the stuff quick.' He pressed £400 of over-thumbed £10 notes into my hand.

My mouth felt dry but I tried to look nonchalant. 'OK, DP, no problem, sounds pretty straightforward.'

Around 1.45 a.m. I slipped out of the crack house. I asked Crystal to come with me for moral support. The road DP had arranged for me to meet Dex in was in the heart of the red light area. I wished he'd chosen somewhere a little less conspicuous. My hands trembled on the steering wheel as I turned into Broughton Road. The houses looked fast asleep and nothing moved. Suddenly a car appeared. I slouched down as far as I could in the driver's seat. I was sure that the car that drove past was an unmarked vice squad car. They thought they were so smart when they travelled incognito – two very straight-looking men in T-shirts in a brand new car. All the women working on the streets recognised them immediately and melted away into the shadows.

I knew that there were lots of people literally crawling up the walls back at the crack house waiting for me to relieve them of their cravings and if I let them and DP down I'd be in serious trouble. The digital clock on the dashboard blinked 2.03 a.m. Where was Dex? Every second lasted a minute. Eventually, at 2.20, a car with no headlights on pulled up alongside DP's car. Two pairs of eyes stared out of the car. I was even more terrified than before. An image of my grandmother flashed up in my brain. I saw her cosily standing over the stove cooking my favourite shepherd's pie. How I wished I was sitting in her kitchen warm and safe instead of meeting up with a strange crack dealer whom I couldn't even see apart from a shining pair of eyes, disembodied from the rest of him in the dark street.

He signalled to me to wait and drove off. I wanted to drive off too but I knew I couldn't leave without the drugs. When I felt that I might die of anxiety, sweat and excess tension, there was a tapping on the side window of the car. He jumped into the back seat, handed me the crack, said under his breath, 'Here's da ting,' grabbed the money and was gone.

Aping the behaviour of dealers I had known, I shoved the crack into my mouth and wedged it inside my cheek. Out of sheer relief rather than because of the humorousness of the situation, Crystal started to laugh, a deep belly laugh that rippled on and on. 'You look like a fat, lopsided hamster,' she said when she could finally get some words out.

That night, with the crack squelching in the alcove of my cheek, I felt very close to her. We drove back to the crack house jubilant and giggling. A cheer went up when we walked through the door and a queue of wild-eyed people held out £10 notes as soon as I'd chopped out and weighed the rocks.

Although I was as desperate as they were to smoke a rock, I suddenly felt like an onlooker who had nothing to do with the crazed cravings all around me. The triumph I had felt as I walked through the door fell away. I no longer saw myself as their saviour; instead I had become their torturer. Their hell was the little white rocks and I was taunting them, tantalising them, with this dementing drug that some of them had done terrible things to raise money for.

My reign as queen of the crack house began majestically but ended in ignominy. At first I felt invincible and adored. I knew that even if I'd had two heads I still would have been loved because all that matters to crack users is getting their crack. But all the same I took the adulation personally. Although they never said anything I could see that the women envied me and would have loved to take my place as crack queen bee.

DP had big plans for me. I was allowed to keep a proportion of the profits and the idea was that before long I would be able to use those profits to buy my own crack to sell in the house, freeing him up to open a new crack house. He dreamed of having a chain of good-quality crack houses which never shut and never ran out of drugs, stretching across south London's back streets like a long, wavy strand of hair.

But I disappointed DP by smoking too much crack to make it in the ruthless, focused world of crack house dealers. During the first few days when DP put me in charge of his crack house I exercised self-restraint to try to impress both DP and the customers. I hardly smoked any crack and kept my mind on the job. But then I began smoking crack 'on duty', partly because it was so available that I was unable to resist temptation and partly because without it I couldn't stay awake round the clock which I needed to be able to do to be a successful saleswoman. As long as I could do the job DP didn't seem to mind me smoking now and again and even when I started smoking more and more of the drug I tried not to do it when he was around. When there were no customers and no DP, though, I smoked all my profits and more, breaking the dealer's golden rule – never get high on your own supply. And before long my feelings of invincibility began to ebb away.

I'd been running the crack house for a few months and I was exhausted from a protracted loss of sleep. For days and nights on end I would be able to grab no more than cat naps because of the relentless demands of customers and DP. The combination of sleep deprivation and crack-induced paranoia made me start believing that DP had set me up in some way and was envious of my success. I became more and more convinced that one night DP would creep up behind me, slide his neat, silver gun out and get rid of me with a clean, surprise shot in the back of the head. Of course he was planning to do nothing of the sort but the more I pondered on my bizarre theory the more convinced I became that my life was in danger if I remained in the crack house. So I did what any paranoid crackhead would do. I bolted with ten rocks and £120, the last few hours' takings, mumbling that I was just popping out for five minutes to buy some cigarettes.

Less than thirty minutes later DP called me. I let the voicemail pick up a message I imagined would be so loud that it might cause my phone to spontaneously combust.

By the time I plucked up the courage to listen to my voicemail later that day, six DP messages had piled up. The first one was velvety soft, cajoling me to return to the crack house with all the money and drugs.

'Come on, Angel, don't leave us like this, come back, please come back.'

Each message got louder and by the sixth one he was roaring down the phone.

'If you don't bring the work and the money back now and I mean NOW you'll never work again in this crack house or any other because you won't be alive enough to work.'

Of course I had no intention of going back. In the end I sold my phone and threw the chip from it away. I wanted to make sure that I couldn't be found. For a few months I led an itinerant life. I slept in a hut off Trafalgar Square for a while and went to crack houses far away from DP's terrain, constantly terrified that I would bump into him and that he would kill me without giving it a second thought. I went back to Soho for a while and picked a few punters up on the streets. I constantly thought about my children but was more ashamed than ever of what I had become. Paul was twelve and Keira was five and I wondered how much they'd changed during the months I'd been away from them. I could no longer imagine a time when I would be mentally and physically presentable enough to hold them in my arms again.

One night I ended up back in south London hunting for punters. It was New Year's Eve 2002. I was feeling particularly melancholy and decided to go back to one of my old haunts. I desperately didn't want to be on the streets. I wanted to get off this miserable treadmill, stop using drugs once and for all and live in a warm, cosy home of my imagination where my children would be sitting smiling on the sofa playing with their Christmas presents. It was at that moment that Patrick's car drew up beside me. Patrick wasn't a person I had known well but in my early twenties I had become very friendly with his partner Jill. I had met her at one of the clubs I used to go to. She had a son called Tom the same age as Paul and the two of them became close. Once I became caught up in the crack house scene, though, we drifted apart, although Tom and Paul remained friends.

Seeing Paul's lovely face and knowing that I had abandoned him so that I could destroy myself was more than I could bear. I vowed that I'd stop using drugs once and for all and that I'd get my children back, and at that moment I would have done absolutely anything to be with them once more. As I ran away from him as fast as my skinny legs and high-heeled boots could carry me I experienced a searing pain inside my head like none I had ever known before. When emotional anguish becomes too overpowering it leaks into the body as a harsh, physical pain. The only solution I could think of was to stopper these feelings with more drugs. I desperately wanted to leave the quicksand of drugs and prostitution behind but I decided that I needed to have a very pure form of oblivion to stop the pain I was feeling before I could tackle all the problems in my life and get my children back. To someone who isn't addicted to any substance this logic seems skewed but to anyone who is dependent on drugs, alcohol, cigarettes or anything else it seems like a perfectly reasonably argument to have with yourself.

To reach that state of oblivion I decided to try heroin for the first time. Nobody offered it to me or tried to persuade me that I'd like it. The decision was entirely my own self-destructive work. The various drugs derived from the poppy are supposed to be the most effective painkillers on earth. I was hopeful that heroin might deaden the pain of losing my children in a way that crack no longer could.

The first time I tried heroin my whole body was suffused with a peaceful glow. I could taste it first of all on my tongue, then all my tastebuds woke up to it, swiftly followed by a warm rush through my veins – liquid safety. Nothing could puncture my bubble of protection once the drug took hold. It gave me a lightness and a heaviness of being, all rolled into one. I could feel my troubles being rinsed away, I had a sensation of being bathed in holy water. My pain was cured (for a while).

The crack high made me feel more alert and more tense. It was more jittery than the cotton-wool, padded-cell feeling that heroin induced. The pleasure I experienced with crack was very fragile, as if the world I'd managed to momentarily push back like a tide was about to come crashing over me, making me retch with the stench of its reality. I loved the ceremony of preparing to inject. Because I was already using so much crack I started using the heroin in equal quantities and developed a habit in record time. Because I was injecting heroin so frequently the veins in my arms collapsed alarmingly quickly and I soon graduated to injecting in my groin, a much more dangerous but more powerful hit.

I developed my own rituals within rituals and soon learnt how to speedball – injecting crack and heroin together. Speedballing is the most dangerous way of all to take illicit drugs. I started off by smoking a small hors d'oeuvres rock of crack followed by a speedball main course, and finally a heroin-only dessert, after which I slumped into a syrupy sleep. I had got to the point where I couldn't bear to use crack without heroin or heroin without crack. Only that specific, intense blend would do.

I remained fearful of bumping into DP but heroin blunted that fear. My anxiety was relegated to the world next door. It was soothing to elbow it out of my immediate world that only consisted of income generation and scoring with very occasional bursts of eating and sleeping. Heroin helped take the edge off the pain of losing my children but no drug in the world could remove that pain entirely.

One day, when I was climbing the stairs to a friend's flat, I saw DP. My scalp tingled with horror and sweat dripped down my spine and between my breasts. I was cornered.

17. DP'S COMMUNITY SERVICE ORDER

Contrary to my nightmare fantasies, DP didn't grab his gun and end my life in a splatter of bullets. He stood, strong and square, opposite me, placed his hands on my shoulders and tutted.

'I'm very, very disappointed in you, Angel,' he said, shaking his head with a fake sad look on his face. 'I really thought you were the sort of girl who could go places. I had big plans for you. Let's go.'

He propelled me very forcefully down the stairs and pushed me violently into his car, the car I had loved so much. The car I had spent so many happy and liberated hours in had suddenly become my prison. He clicked the central locking on. When we arrived back at the crack house, he pulled me out of the car, made me run up the stairs and then pushed me inside. The atmosphere had completely changed. Menace hung in the air like yellow fog. The sofa had been slashed with a knife and the stuffing drizzled out like fluffy blood, the TV was gone and the place was filthy. I didn't recognise many of the faces but all of them seemed to be silently growling at me.

DP led me roughly into the bedroom and once we were inside he locked the door decisively. I glanced at the window. The flat was on the tenth floor and I knew that any plan to jump was doomed.

'Where's ma money, Angel?' he asked slowly and evenly. There was no trace of anger in his voice but I knew it was crouching in his stomach like a jack in the box just waiting for the lid to be removed.

I shrugged and said nothing. My eyes cast down in the hope that the missing money might suddenly rise up from the carpet.

'You know I've got to hurt you now, don't you?' he said.

Again I remained silent. I was paralysed by fear. He raised his hand. I cried and cowered. He hit me so hard across the head that I fell backwards onto the bed. By now I was in severe withdrawal. I moaned and shivered in a way that DP could see was not caused by a blow to the head. I think he had probably been planning to continue taking swipes at me but seeing how ill and pathetic I looked, he stepped back.

'What's da matter wid you, Angel? You look like you're about to die on me.'

'I've got a habit, DP,' I told him, quaking. 'I'm withdrawing and I'm in agony. It's like the worst flu you can imagine.'

He kissed his teeth in frustration at my stupidity for getting involved with heroin.

'Angel, you owe me money and you ran my crack house better than anyone else I've employed. We've got a problem here. You need to repay your debt but you're not going to be able to work in that state. You've got to get rid of that nasty smack habit. I can't have no seller of mine using that kind of thing. You'll be drooping in front of the customers and they'll all rob you blind. You need to be on the ball to sell and remember what I always told you about treating your body with respect. I'm going to clear that stuff out of your system and then you can work for me again.'

The room he had taken me into was Jimmy's mother's bedroom. It was a small bedroom and was in a much better state than the rest of the place. It had a bed with a lilac duvet cover on it, a blond wood bedside table, a laminate wooden floor and a wall cupboard.

'Welcome to DP's detox,' he said, almost smiling for the first time. 'I'm sorry, Angel, but I'm afraid I'm going to have to lock you in and reduce your heroin gradually. Then when you're clean we can get to work.'

I was appalled. I had no intention of giving up heroin and didn't like DP taking charge of my life in this way. He went out, locking the door behind him, and returned half an hour later with a small wrap of heroin and some foil for me to smoke it off. He also put on the bedside table a carton of carrot juice, a couple of his favourite tofu burgers, some green salad in a small Tupperware box and a couple of magazines where almost every page had a shiny-toothed model extolling the benefits of living a healthy life.

'I've bought you some good, fresh food from John's [the local wholefood shop] and some interesting reading material to help you pass the time. Just eat, sleep and relax and in a few days your body will be clear of those evil opiates,' he said.

He gave me an 'I'm in control, don't even think about making a run for it' smile, walked out of the room and locked the door behind him. 'If you want to make it in the world of business, you have to apply yourself, Angel,' were his parting words to me. I believe that although I was a business asset to DP and owed him money, those weren't the only reasons he was forcing a detox on me. Other people in the crack house told me that DP really cared about me and that it upset him greatly seeing me in that state. It didn't, of course, upset him enough to stop selling drugs.

'Let me go! I don't want to make it in business. I just want to be left alone to take whatever drugs I want to take in peace,' I shouted feebly at the closed door.

DP was the kind of man who, once he had a plan, would not deviate from it.

True to his word, he visited me twice a day delivering the kind of inedible, healthy food that reminded me of the worst excesses of my mother's cooking. The amounts of heroin he handed over decreased and decreased over a five-day period. On the sixth day there were tofu burgers again but no drugs.

'It's time, Angel. You've reduced to almost nothing; your withdrawal shouldn't feel too bad.'

I hated to admit that he was right. The withdrawal had been survivable. I curled up under the lilac duvet cover, shivered and sweated a little and slept with the help of some paracetamol. The time had dragged with minimal human contact apart from DP's food and drug deliveries to my bedside but I actually quite enjoyed lying in a tranquil space knowing that on the other side of the door people squabbled over crumbs of crack and tried to bargain with dealers to get a rock for £9.50 instead of £10. Not having to constantly hustle for my drugs money had been a real holiday for me. I slept for twelve hours and would have slept longer had I not been interrupted by a sickeningly cheerful DP.

'Good morning, Angel, rise and shine. Today is your first day back as deputy CEO of DP's Crack House Inc. Get your arse in gear, girl, we've got work to do and you've got a serious debt to pay off.'

DP ushered me through the living room, where a few revellers from the previous night were about to leave, and took me into the kitchen.

'You ready to start working for me again, then?'

I nodded. I really didn't want to work for DP any longer. Since the age of thirteen I had constantly moved forward, involving myself in increasingly dangerous and risky things. When I first worked for DP I was doing something new and exciting but the thought of returning to something I had run away from seemed like an admission of total failure. I wanted to keep on moving forward, running further and further away from myself. The retrograde step of working for DP again meant that I risked having to turn around and face myself.

The feeling that some evil force had invaded the crack house remained with me. A few days after I started selling drugs for DP again, one of the smokers suddenly turned violent. It happened quite frequently that men who walked through the door of the flat looking perfectly reasonably could flip over into violent paranoia as soon as they started smoking crack. Without warning the man pushed an armchair against the living room door, barricading in me, the doorman and a female crack smoker. Then he picked up the big, jagged piece of glass that I cut the crack up with.

'Anyone who moves gets this in the neck,' he said. A vein on the side of his neck was quivering with rage and perhaps excitement too. He was a small, white man with mousy, balding hair and stained brown trousers, greasy with dirt and sweat. I wondered if he felt inadequate in life and was holding us hostage as a way of boosting his self-esteem. I unfolded my arms, which had been clamped around my ribs. I was terrified that he was going to slit our throats with the glass one by one.

'Don't you dare move,' he said when he saw my arms change position. The three of us sat bolt upright with our hands by our sides like petrified Victorian schoolchildren waiting for the headmaster to cane us all in turn.

I kept myself going by thinking that his paranoia would wear off eventually and he would let us go. After about an hour he grudgingly moved the armchair away from the door, placed the piece of glass back on the table and casually walked out of the crack house.

As well as working in the crack house for DP I spent time on the streets picking up punters. If they were men who were interested in smoking crack I'd suggest that we went back to the crack house to 'do business'. The idea was that they would become regular customers spending money on both me and crack. On one of my night time trawls of Clapham Common in search of punters when the crack house was quiet, I met John, a kindly looking old man. He was one of the unlikeliest people to find his way into a crack house. I was trying to redeem my battered reputation with DP by supplementing my work in the crack house by bringing as many crack-smoking customers back to the house as possible. The more time they spent in a crack house the more money they parted with. He was walking two springer spaniels and was immaculately dressed in well-to-do pensioner clothes – shirt and tie and cardigan with freshly pressed trousers and carefully polished shoes.

My first thought when he approached me was that he was lost or that he wanted to know the time. But he had no such things on his mind.

'Could you help me to score?' he said in a rather frail voice.

Using crack makes you doubly wary, first because it's illegal so there's always the prospect of getting caught, and second because the drug makes you paranoid and distrustful of everyone who crosses your path. I couldn't believe that this soft and fragile pensioner really wanted to buy drugs.

'Are you an undercover cop in disguise or something?' I asked sharply.

'No, no, no, my dear. Please. Could you help me? I really would like to go and have a smoke.'

He spoke with a colonial English accent like one of those upper-class grandfather figures I remembered from my childhood reading fairytales for BBC children's story-time slots. By this time I was disbelieving rather than suspicious but I took him back to the house. I had a room there which was less filthy and chaotic than the rest of the house although it was still grimy and sparsely furnished. He proved to be a seasoned crack smoker and stayed for nine hours, smoking constantly and expecting me to do the same. It was a Monday night and the crack house was quiet. It was the day before many people collected their benefit cheques so people's finances were at their lowest ebb.

As John smoked, he talked. 'I'm dying of cancer, my dear, and I feel that I'd like to try out all sorts of pleasurable things before I die. Smoking crack is certainly one of life's pleasures.' I was amazed that he seemed to have the stamina and strength to go on smoking such a powerful drug for so long. I'd seen younger, healthier people than him succumb to crack-induced heart attacks or strokes and I was mentally running through my options if he collapsed on me. People in crack houses didn't generally call ambulances for obvious reasons. Maybe I'd call a taxi, see if he had any money left in his pocket to pay for it and then drop him off at the door of the local Accident and Emergency department. But the cancer didn't seem to have dented his obviously cast-iron constitution. He remained lucid and vertical.

The more he talked, the more lonely he sounded. His soft brown eyes fastened on to mine and somehow I couldn't look away. I said very little, just listened, nodded and smoked.

'You seem such a kind, gentle girl, my dear. Would you come and live with me? I'd look after you, you know. I've got a bit of life in me yet despite my grim prognosis. Have you heard of the famous line from the poet Dylan Thomas: "Rage, rage against the dying of the light"? That's exactly how I feel. But it's getting dark too quickly and it's so lonely doing it all by myself.'

'I couldn't possibly leave everything here just like that,' I said, trying to soothe him out of the idea. 'My life is here in this house now.' For me the whole process of smoking crack was about emotional distance and disengagement from others: my chemical buffer zone. I didn't mind opening my legs for paying customers but I couldn't bear it when they tried to get into my soul.

He smiled sadly and got ready to go home. Dawn was breaking and the sky was an impassioned red.

'Look, the sun's going to shine brightly today. Maybe today will be a better day for you,' I said, trying to find a way of giving him some spiritual succour that didn't involve surrendering myself. One of the benefits of losing myself to drugs was that I could no longer feel anything very much. But this old man had managed to burrow beyond the layers of crack insulation to excavate feelings I didn't know I still had. He had unearthed sympathy for a fellow human in distress. As I looked out of the window and watched him walking slowly and deliberately down the street, tears came, for his ebbing life and for what mine had become.

18. FATHER

I never found out why the man DP wanted me to visit was called Father. At first I thought he was some sort of Godfather linchpin in DP's drug-selling empire but in the end I decided he was just an extremely good customer, another pensioner who liked his crack, and that he was possibly related to DP, hence the respectful form of address.

I was even more surprised to find that Father was a lover of crack than I had been when John the cancer man approached me. Father lived in a sheltered housing complex for elderly people. DP lived close by in a flat opposite a police station, a strategic double bluff, perhaps. Sometimes he stayed the night at Father's and slept on the sofa although I never knew why. Later on I decided that having access to an old person's flat in a sheltered housing complex was an ideal bolthole for DP whenever he needed to lie low or allow some money or drugs which had become too 'hot' to cool down for a few days. Although my skin colour was different from Father's, I think DP hoped everyone would assume I was his granddaughter paying a dutiful visit.

Father was a slight, wizened Jamaican man. I guessed that he was in his mid-seventies. His flat was tiny and furnished in a traditional way. A table covered with a lace tablecloth was the centrepiece of the room and his walls were filled with photographs of his grandchildren and other members of his extended family. On his sideboard was a huge St James bible. It was open but I couldn't see which bit Father had been reading. As usual, DP wasted no breath on explaining to me what his relationship with Father was and why we were visiting him.

'This is Angel,' he said gruffly to Father once we'd been ushered inside. 'Angel by name, Angel by nature, aren't ya, girl?'

I nodded to Father and he grinned at me and winked.

'DP will tell you I'm very fond of da ladies, particularly da ones who look like angels and talk like angels,' said Father. He cupped my elbow in the palm of his hand. I felt very uneasy. DP took out a big lump of crack, a roll of clingfilm and his scales. As DP weighed out and parcelled up tiny pieces of crack, all the crumbs were pushed over to Father, who methodically tipped them into a glass pipe he fetched from a dark wood sideboard. He handed a pipe to me and DP gave me some crack and got up to leave.

'I'll be back for you in about an hour, Angel,' said DP. I presumed that my job was to entertain Father in whatever way he wanted to be entertained for as long as he smoked as much crack as he wanted to smoke. Unsure how much of a hold Father had over DP, I decided I'd better fall into line with whatever Father wanted to do.

As he prepared his pipe, half-moon glasses slipping down the bridge of his nose, he became very serious and focused. Once he started smoking he donned a trilby hat and sunglasses and stripped down to his underpants. I feared the worst but rather than demanding sex he put on an Ashanti CD and showed me his miraculous powers of making his penis wiggle in time to the music. I laughed politely. He had the crack and he had DP on his side so all I could do was play the role of the obedient, adoring little woman.

When the hour was up, DP reappeared and handed me my coat.

'Everything OK, Father?' he asked.

'Yes, yes, boy, perfectly, thank you.'

'I'll see you next week then. Let's go, Angel, we've got work to do.'

DP was very driven. He never seemed to take a day off and was forever focused on some crack-centred task or other. After that first meeting, DP took me round to Father's house regularly, sometimes with one or more other young women.

Father was often benign but as I discovered he had a nasty side too.

He acted as occasional jailer for DP. Once, the doorman took some of DP's crack when the dealer's back was temporarily turned and offered some of it to me. DP rarely sat in the house or sullied himself with dealing. He was a born delegator and he only usually popped in to deliver crack or to collect the takings. I assumed that the rest of the time he was striking business deals to enhance his supply of drugs or honing his pristine muscles. When he arrived to collect the night's takings, he saw straight away that they were £50 short. Like a buzzard equipped with a telepathic microchip, he circled the doorman and me.

'Wocha done with ma money?' he said grimly. The doorman and I hung our heads. There was no point telling some elaborate tale of being robbed at knifepoint or of having the barrel of a gun pushed against our bellies.

'Right, I'll deal with you separately,' he said to the doorman. 'I can't run an efficient business if I can't trust my staff.'

A hard-faced man with uncomfortably large biceps stood impassively next to DP.

'Sort him out.' He nodded to the man, who grabbed the doorman and proceeded to kick and beat him without moving a muscle of his face. DP had a different punishment in mind for me. He took me roughly by the arm and led me to his car.

'Father can deal with you,' he said. He seemed far angrier with me than he had been with the doorman. We arrived at Father's flat and DP nodded wordlessly to Father, who looked at me gravely through his slipping-down-the-nose spectacles. As far as I knew, DP hadn't called Father since discovering my transgression and gave no explanation now of what had happened. It seemed as if the two of them could communicate by telepathy.

Father led me to the bedroom and locked me in. I howled and begged to be released. It was my twenty-ninth birthday and it seemed particularly unjust to be punished so severely. Apart from this, in my opinion, very minor transgression, I'd been DP's loyal servant, bringing customers to the house and helping him to network. He understood the drugs business but he needed contacts. In order to make that kind of enterprise work, acumen and contacts are needed in equal measure.

'Let me out, let me out!' I banged on the door.

'No, you can stay in there and reflect on your sins,' Father shouted through the door. 'You're just a catty little rock star.' Both the terms 'catty' and 'rock star' were used in a pejorative sense in crack house circles and referred to users of the drug.

I lay down and tried to sleep. I was as furious with myself for blotting my copybook as I was with Father and DP. Later Father relented and unlocked the bedroom door. He had a lodger called Chantelle who was a prostitute. She had become skinny and withered from using too much crack for too long. Like heroin, crack was a drug which virtually guaranteed dramatic weight loss. Father offered us both some crack. Then Chantelle insisted on going out to raise money for more crack.

She took me with her in Father's car and somehow, without me noticing, managed to pick up an expensive mobile phone which I'd left on the seat beside me and took it with her into a block of flats. I had assumed she had gone into the flats to 'do business' with a punter to raise some money for the next couple of rocks but in fact she'd gone to a dealer's flat and exchanged my phone for crack.

'How could you do that to me?' I ranted. 'Don't you have any sense of solidarity with a fellow working girl? I wouldn't dream of stitching you up like that.'

Chantelle was driving and appeared not to hear. As far as she was concerned I had crossed the line with DP and was fair game for any sort of punishment that she and Father decided to mete out to me. At that moment I hated every atom that made up the crack lifestyle. I felt used and devastated and worthless and vowed to get out. If only I had.

I had been spending most of my time in DP's crack house but after the crack-stealing incident I decided I needed a few days away from the place to give resentments and frayed tempers a chance to cool. I had paid my debt to DP and was no longer a wanted woman. This time I drifted away from DP in a vague and amicable way.

'I'm taking a bit of a break, DP,' I told him. 'I'll see you around.'

DP shrugged. He didn't seem to mind letting me go. I'd failed to realise my business potential and he seemed to have lost interest in nurturing me. Crack-centred relationships are like that. The normal social conventions are suspended and people can become vital to each other's existence very quickly but then sever connections even more quickly than they were forged. I'd also lost touch with Crystal. Our love affair with crack was a destructive common interest too far and in the end it drove us apart. We decided we'd be better off self-destructing separately than together. Although we'd shared a bed, a toothbrush and all our clothes and had felt the burning heat of each other's souls, we drifted apart very suddenly. I missed her sometimes and reflected on the way I, who had once been the wallflower of the crack house, while Crystal had been the confident one, had risen to the dizzy heights of running one of the establishments I had once feared setting foot in.

I began living in a series of different squats and crack houses and various places that were somewhere between the two. I was lost during this period, quite literally, and led a nocturnal, nomadic existence. I stayed away from the streets during the hours of daylight. I was frightened that flecks of reality might graze my skin. No one knew where I was. There were occasional sightings of me but in the world of nether regions that I inhabited no one was ever sure whether a whispered word was truth or urban myth. I liked the anonymity. I felt free of all responsibility. For the first time in their lives I missed my children's birthdays. I went back to heroin, used more crack, stockpiled cans of strong lager and got through the day. It dulled the physical pain of being away from my children but it didn't stop me feeling like an abject failure. As well as disappearing from my children's lives for almost a year, I stopped calling my mother. Frantic with worry, she reported me missing. I was known to the vice squad, who had once chased me across Brixton Hill, taken a Polaroid picture of me and demanded my name and address (I gave an old one) for their records. But the missing person computers and the vice squad computers obviously didn't talk to each other and nobody discovered me.

My mother travelled regularly from her home in Bristol to Brixton and Streatham where she knew I had spent time. She paced Brixton Hill clutching a laminated poster with my picture on it. She stopped people in the street, begging them for information about me. I was far too wrapped up in my own misery and self-loathing to give much thought to the pain I was causing those who loved me. I knew that my mother had no idea whether I was alive or dead. She told me later that as well as walking the streets – some sort of eerie parallel with what I was doing – she went into pubs where she thought I might go. One of the people in the pub gave her an address of a filthy, flea-infested flat in Wandsworth that I had lived in for a while. She told me, when we did finally reunite, that she asked the police to go into the squat to look for clues about me and they emerged surrounded by a halo of fleas. She was appalled and said she'd never seen anything like it in her life.

Eliciting information from some of the women who worked on the street was another part of my mother's strategy to track me down. Talking to them did nothing to allay my mother's fears for my welfare.

'They looked like walking corpses,' she said to me later, putting her hand over her mouth at the memory of it. But thoughts about how I coped with prostitution or how many drugs I took were not uppermost in her mind. All she wanted to know was whether I was still alive.

'But nobody could tell me for sure. I felt as if I was on the outside staring in at some sort of hellish underworld,' she said.

My mother's efforts came to nothing. I continued skulking around during the hours of darkness. When people choose to get lost they're very hard to find. A couple of people I knew said to me that a woman had been walking around asking people if they knew me. She hadn't told them she was my mother and at the time it never occurred to me that it was she who was looking for me. I was far too scared of facing her or anyone else at that time. All I could think about was how angry everyone would be with me and how much everyone would hate me. The thought of being chastised by my mother and other family members was too terrifying for me to contemplate.

Darren and I had told the children that Mummy wasn't well in her head and needed some time by herself to get better. I hoped that that flimsy explanation would be robust enough to keep them going until I was ready to return to them.

I started going to other crack houses, all different yet all the same. I became tired of the manipulative tricks that some of the house owners played on dealers and customers. One man, Timmy, who allowed his flat to be used as a crack house, used crutches to get around. Crack house etiquette was to buy a pipe of crack for the house owner on arrival, in the same way that the middle classes proffer wine or chocolates when they turn up for a dinner party in suburbia. If Timmy felt he wasn't getting enough crack he lay on the floor screaming, legs flailing in the air like a two-year-old having a tantrum, and threatened to call the police unless he got as much crack as he wanted and got it now. It usually worked. Some house owners slipped the fuse out of the electricity box, plunging everyone into darkness if things weren't going their way on the freebie front. Some were strategic about allowing their houses to be used. They would tolerate it for so long, benefitting from a steady supply of drugs, then would call the police and say that they were a vulnerable tenant who was helpless in the face of a takeover by vicious crack dealers. Several people I knew secured housing transfers to more salubrious properties that way. The media report vulnerable people with mental health problems having their flats forcibly 'repossessed' by crack dealers. That may have happened but I never saw it. In my experience flat and house owners colluded with dealers to a greater or lesser extent.

One crack house was owned by a paranoid schizophrenic woman called Penelope who carried a long, black-handled kitchen knife in the waistband of her trousers. The house looked as ransacked as any other crack house but there was one room that she kept locked. I thought of the story of Bluebeard and wondered what was behind the padlocked door.

For some reason Penelope seemed to like me and one evening invited me to come and pay homage in the room.

She had a soft, dreamy voice and I was never certain if she was telling the truth or living out an unbalanced fantasy.

She opened the door to reveal a beautifully decorated nursery. It was a diametrical opposite to the rest of the crack house. All was order and cleanliness and soothing pastel furnishings. In the corner was a cot with white bars and three little mobiles dancing above it.

'I lost a baby to cot death,' she confided. 'But I preserved this room as a shrine for my lost child.'

She solemnly asked me and a select group of people to come and sit on the floor of the nursery with her and smoke crack. 'Let's all reflect on baby Sarah's short but beautiful life,' she said, like a vicar beginning a lesson in church. It was a surreal and rather eerie experience.

The world of crack was populated by many different types of people. There were the sociable types who hung around crack houses in groups, the loners who used crack to give them a sense of belonging when other worlds rejected them, the mentally ill who wanted to escape from the tormenting innards of their heads and there was Dave. I'm not sure which category Dave fitted into. Probably a bit of all of the above. It was Dave whom I turned to when I needed a place to lie low.

He was sitting, beaming, on a park bench and instantly recognising a kindred drug spirit, I sat down next to him and we started chatting. Dave offered me a place to stay and before I had seen what it was like I accepted his offer. He lived in a tiny top floor flat in a tower block. It was piled high from floor to ceiling with junk he had collected from builders' skips.

The water had long been disconnected and I made various surreal findings including piles of human faeces sitting in a frying pan on the stove and urine sloshing around the kitchen bin. I felt the flat was too dirty to breathe in. The only part of his living room that wasn't crammed with junk was a stained mattress in the middle of the room which served as bed by night and sofa by day. Dave became my willing injecting partner.

He was one of the kindest, gentlest people I had met. He had a set routine and left his flat every lunchtime dressed in a shabby overcoat and a fishing hat to get a subsidised meal at a local homeless day centre. He had no electricity and used tealights when it got dark. I never understood how he managed to avoid setting the place on fire. Dave frequently overdosed on heroin; I think the oblivion appealed to him. We didn't talk much but every so often he said in a slurred and deliberate voice: 'Always remember that life is good and that God is good. God wouldn't have put drugs on this earth if he hadn't wanted us to get pleasure from them, would he?'

'I guess you're right, Dave,' I said, keen to be emollient towards my temporary landlord although I wasn't at all sure about his theory. Despite his shambling gait he was only in his forties. I stayed with him for a few days and soon afterwards I heard he'd died of an overdose. I was happy for him because I'm sure that he had wanted to die and that that's how he wanted to go. During my brief time at Dave's flat I never really considered that there was anything out of the ordinary about him or his surroundings. It was a sign of how far I'd fallen.

19. THE STRANGE SHAPES AND SIZES OF PUNTERS

I had abandoned my hairdressing career when I handed the children over to Darren and at that point began to work regularly in street prostitution. My final year in the sex industry was my busiest of all. I was slipping further and further away from hope then and selling my body was a cornerstone of my descent. All the women working on the streets followed more or less the same template. I only came across one or two street-based women who didn't use Class A drugs, although the majority of women working in saunas, flats and massage parlours rarely used any drugs at all.

Working on the streets, we would run to our dealer to buy ten of brown and ten of white, which we'd smoke and inject before racing back to find more punters to earn another £20. We were all hamsters on a wheel. We hated the drugs we needed to survive the hell of the punters. Rapes were common but women rarely reported them for fear of being dealt with unsympathetically by the police or, worse, having the rape dismissed and instead being arrested for soliciting. I spent some of my time in crack houses, ingratiating myself with the house dealers by bringing in punters who would have sex with me and spend copious amounts of money on crack. Prostitutes were always vulnerable to being robbed in crack houses because they often had more money than everyone else and of course nobody ever called the police. I loathed the punter/drugs/punter/drugs treadmill but there didn't seem to be any alternative. I remember walking down Brixton High Road one day in a snow blizzard. I couldn't see in front of me; I needed money for my next fix but saw no punters. I wished that the snow, as it settled against my cold skin, would melt me out of existence.

Some of my punters were rich, others were poor, some smelled of clean washing and cologne, but most of stale beer, cigarettes and sweat. They were all different yet all the same. Usually they were overwhelmed with an urgency to relieve themselves inside me as if they were rushing for a train. Almost all had no desire to talk either before or after doing the deed.

I could usually spot the married ones because they hung their heads a little lower than the rest when we agreed on a price and their shirts were more neatly pressed. For them the sex was much more of a 999 affair than it was with the unattached. They were speedier than the rest, which I preferred because it meant I was earning a higher rate per minute than I was with the nuisance men who wanted to take their time or, worse, chat both as foreplay and during those post-coital minutes when all I wanted to do was run off to the nearest dealer or crack house. The married men tended to appear earlier in the evening so that they could get home and be tucked up in bed beside their wives at an unsuspicious hour.

As the evenings wore on, the punters tended to become more unsavoury and less part of so-called respectable society – loners, crack addicts, warped insomniacs. Fortunately most men didn't want to chat, or to tell me anything about their backgrounds, which was the way I wanted things to be. I would have liked to draw up a list of instructions to my punters, chalked on a blackboard and accompanying me to whichever street corner I happened to be standing on. At the top would be no talking about jobs, wives, kids, politics or football, followed by keeping their faces as far away from me as possible so that I didn't have to inhale halitosis fumes. Bonus points would be awarded for having sex at fast-forward speed (punters may be rewarded with a half smile for that because none of us working girls smiled very much) and, most important of all, no trying to drive the price down because they knew it was late and cold and I was desperate because I was withdrawing from heroin.

The customers' backgrounds and circumstances were diverse but their penises in action were more or less the same. Few seemed bothered about contracting a sexually transmitted infection and most would have jumped at the chance to throw their condom to the winds. One man, who drove a battered old Range Rover and looked moneyed, used to pull up alongside me and another woman called Kayleigh, who often worked close to me.

'Evenin', girls, I can pay £120 each if you'll both do it without a condom.' Desperate though we were for the cash, we declined. Various pieces of research have found very low levels of sexually transmitted infections among sex workers. Protecting ourselves wasn't rocket science and we were far more at risk of being contaminated by them than they were by us. Perhaps they knew that and that's why they badgered us so persistently for condom-free sex.

Dealers sometimes crossed over into punter territory but they struck different kinds of bargains. They often flirted outrageously with the women selling sex. It was never about us, always about reinforcing their own macho supremacy at the top of the crack house tree. Sometimes one would affectedly move a piece of hair out of my eyes or drape an arm casually around my bony shoulder.

A 'rock for a fuck' deal was often available but some of the dealers were quite fastidious about having sex with me or one of the others. One insisted on wearing two condoms.

'Just to be sure, Angel, just to be sure. Don't go taking no offence now.'

I was lucky enough to encounter very little violence from my customers. I always kept my eyes fixed on the door locks of cars and as long as the driver didn't flick them to the lock position I knew that I was a second or two away from escaping to freedom. For me there was an odd paradox about selling sex. Sometimes, while the men banged themselves rhythmically against my hip bones and squelched inside their condoms, I thought with pity of their wives or girlfriends enduring the same thing but for no payment, and felt empowered. But at the same time the sheer repetitiveness of the actions imposed on my body made me despise men and despise myself for being a human receptacle for the physical urges which appeared to operate entirely independently of male minds. After the physical violence I had suffered in my relationships with Leroy and Billy, my self-esteem around men was shockingly low but somehow prostitution restored it. I was no longer frightened of men the way I had been during those relationships. While their overwhelming need to keep on parting company with millions of sperm made men physically powerful, it also made them vulnerable. When I was sitting or lying over or under them, I often thought, 'So that's really all there is to you, a body programmed to push sperm out of you and into me. You're pathetic, you're boring, hurry up and get on with it. I have no interest in you apart from your money.'

Sometimes, to appease their own consciences rather than out of any genuine concern for me, they said, 'You're such a lovely girl – why are you doing this work? I'm sure you'd do very well if you got yourself a proper job.' Their pity irritated me. 'Don't waste precious minutes feeling sorry for me,' I shouted inside my head. 'Just shut up and let me go. I'm doing this to get your money to buy my drugs.'

I tried out different looks with my customers. Sometimes I gazed blankly at them while I giggled silently to myself. I'm sure most of them mistook that look for adoration. I enjoyed the acting dimension of the job. The more coy or vulnerable I appeared to be with them, the more powerful I felt inside. Unwittingly they fuelled me with a very private fire. They might have thought that they were in control but in reality they rarely were. One time when men had absolute supremacy, though, was when they pulled over in their cars, looked you up and down and decided whether they were going to pay money to shoot a bundle of sperm into you or not. Whenever I looked ill with withdrawal, they tried to drop the price from £20 to £10.

'It's a tenner or nothing,' some of them would say. 'You take your choice, love,' some of them said cruelly, enjoying my discomfiture and witnessing my frail, shivering, aching body.

Some of my clients were young, beautiful black men who were in long-term, settled relationships with women they said were attractive and successful.

'My girl would kill me with her bare hands if she ever discovered that I was straying,' said one man.

Another was sheepish and monosyllabic and I guessed from that that he was attached.

I did have a couple of favourite customers. They were defined by their kindness and straightforwardness. One man, who told me his name was Eric, was a cabbie and a painter and decorator. We chatted as we drove to a particularly quiet side street, flanked by overhanging trees on one side of the road. When we parked under those trees I felt as if I was an eye and the trees were a heavy lashed eyelid pulling over me. The backs of cars were the most common temporary boudoirs but venues ranged from opulent Knightsbridge flats to smelly bin cupboards on council estates.

For a few months I worked for an escort agency. It promised high-class escorts who spoke several languages and made perfect companions for business dinners and trips to the theatre. I don't think the few words of German I could remember from my childhood or being able to say hello and goodbye in Portugese counted as 'several languages', nor would I have felt comfortable at a business dinner with my crack pipe pushed into my pocket. But the lack of these attributes didn't seem to matter to the customers. In the end they wanted more or less the same thing as the men who screwed me in the council estate bin cupboards.

The agency was run from a scruffy room in a rundown flat by a fifty-something woman with bleached, set hair who smelt of sweat and sickly perfume. A cigarette dripping too much ash perpetually dangled in either her mouth or her hand. I wondered what the customers who answered the advert for refined, high-class escorts speaking five languages would have thought had they visited the 'escort agency' in person. After all, they were buying into a fantasy of sorts.

One of the crack dealers I knew happened to live in the flat across the road from the escort agency. I decided it was fate, part of my drugs destiny. It was a very short trip from the escort agency to collect my money to his flat to part with it.

The escort agency customers were generally more moneyed than the street punters and often a lot less straightforward. Many of them used cocaine. One customer was a diamond merchant. Judging by his luxurious flat he had earned millions. He had all the latest designer furnishings including tiny lights that studded the skirting boards and could be dimmed or made brighter. He paid me and the other women he ordered £300 an hour and usually wanted us to stay for three hours. He didn't want to have sex with us but after snorting prodigious quantities of cocaine off a small mirror wanted to watch us pulling each other along on a lead, dressed in stilettos and black PVC macs. He also wanted to insert a variety of objects into us and to watch us urinate on each other. He fed us large amounts of cocaine; I don't think any of us would have agreed to such unpleasant and degrading commands without the anaesthesia of the drugs, even for £300 an hour.

Despite my drug use I still looked reasonably presentable. I was slim but not emaciated and because I'd only been injecting heroin for a few months my track marks were concealable with thick foundation cream. One punter noticed the marks on my arms where I had slashed myself and however hard I tried to convince him that they were scratches inflicted by my (imaginary) playful cat he refused to believe me. It turned out that he was a medical student at a hospital in south London. He seemed pleased to have 'diagnosed' me, refused to have sex with me in my vulnerable state but instead spent more than an hour talking to me about what he thought my problems were.

I divulged little and in the end he sent me away saying: 'Please get some help, you really can beat this self-harming business, you know.'

Perhaps he felt good about switching from predator to counselor. I promised him I'd get help and eased myself out of the door as quickly as I could. I had no intention of getting any sort of help and was upset that the pep talk had taken so long.

One man I saw a couple of times used to book a room at a Travelodge in central London for us to meet. He was a stern, slight, immaculate-looking man.

'Strip off and lie on the bed,' he ordered in a quiet, commanding tone, removing his own clothes and donning a pair of surgical gloves. I feared the worst but in fact he wanted neither to have sex with me nor to insert anything unpleasant into any of my orifices. He simply wanted to play doctors with me. He examined every part of my body carefully then told me I could dress and go. He paid £180 for half an hour and it was the easiest money I'd ever earned. He seemed quite informed in the way that he examined me and I wondered if he was a frustrated doctor who was allowed within the confines of the Travelodge to examine a patient the way he longed to examine them in his surgery.

I still conflate men and punters. I feel angry at the way they look at me when I'm sitting in a cafe drinking coffee, undressing me with their eyes from head to toe. I become enraged when they sit next to me on a bus spreading their legs out so that one leg invades my space and touches my leg. That's part of the damage caused by prostitution. I hope that the further away I move from the days of selling my body, the less I'll see men in that way. Before I became involved in prostitution proper in my late twenties I had regarded men as a means of making me feel better about myself. Although the relationships never lasted, in the early days of my time with Jerome, Leroy and Darren I felt loved and cosseted and important. Once I started working on the streets the brief but pleasurable feelings I'd experienced with men evaporated. Instead I felt that I had no value as a woman unless I was giving something to a man or doing something for him. I was no longer worth anything simply as me. Seeing so many men naked made me think, that stripped of their smart or shabby clothes, that's all men are underneath, self seekers who want to take and take from women. When I left prostitution my attitude softened a little. I remained wary of men and probably will feel that way for the rest of my life but I regained some optimism that not all men are equally bad. However, unlike during the times when I entered relationships solely on the basis of a man showing some interest and affection in me, my standards are now very exacting. To date no man has been given the 'all clear' with my finely honed bullshit detector but perhaps some day one will.

While my chaotic lifestyle continued punters were a necessary evil for me but I had begun to hanker after something different. Other women who worked on the streets had told me about a project called Spires, a church-based organisation which offered a range of services to homeless and vulnerable people, including clothes, hot meals, outreach services offering condoms and clean needles to street sex workers, referrals to drug treatment facilities and help with finding housing. Various people had recommended the project to me and sitting bored stiff in a crack house one day I decided to take a look. A blonde, bubbly woman called Denise greeted me.

'Should I fetch you a dinner?' she asked kindly. I nodded.

'I'll do an assessment for you if you like,' she said casually after I'd wolfed down minced meat, potatoes and carrots, the first proper meal I'd had in weeks, and food which reminded me of meals at my grandmother's house.

In the course of the assessment, in which she asked what my main areas of need were, I answered, 'Giving up drugs, then getting some permanent housing, then getting my kids back, in that order,' and she said something which startled me. It was different from the platitudes I'd heard from other drugs workers.

She leaned forward and said quietly: 'You know, if you want to stop using drugs, you can. I did it.'

I looked at her, happy and normal and breaking off every so often to take a call from her children, who asked her what time she'd be home and what she was cooking for supper that night. I was suddenly flooded with optimism. I wanted what Denise had and for the first time I believed that it was possible to get it. Denise continued to help, support and encourage me more than she'll ever know. I was standing on one side of the abyss and she had safely crossed to the other side. She stood patiently and, with a strong, outstretched arm, helped me cross too.

20. A CRACK HOUSE WITH STAFF

Staff at homeless hostels promise all manner of life-changing services to the people they look after. Some deliver but many don't. Hostels receive large sums of housing benefit for each individual they accommodate but too many serve as incubators for damaging behaviours. People I've known have launched careers in prostitution as a result of being shown the ropes by others in hostels. And as for drug habits, hostels are among the best places to develop a drug habit, worsen an existing habit or relapse after a fragile period of recovery. Peer pressure in these places is overwhelming. Anyone who has overcome addiction may be seen as a threat to those who are still using. For an addict, encountering someone who has stopped using heightens their own sense of failure. To make themselves feel less insecure some try to drag any recent quitters back down as quickly as possible.

'Don't think you're not a cat like the rest of us, because you are,' was a common taunt to anyone who was trying to stop using drugs.

Denise secured me a place in a hostel where I lived for several months. It ticked all of the bad boxes but when I arrived there my heart leapt.

Inside yellowing paint was crumbling off the walls. Some of the residents who had contracted hepatitis C as a result of sharing drug paraphernalia had skin the same colour. There were bare floorboards and an unpleasant taste of chaos in the air, at times bordering on pandemonium, as residents wandered up and down stairs looking either frantic or glazed depending on which drugs they'd been taking.

The feel of the place reminded me of a crack house except that hovering in the background there were staff. These people who ran the hostel did little to challenge the status quo. They didn't bother erasing the drug dealers' phone numbers which were scratched on the wall of the public phone box in the reception area, they didn't challenge the dealers who crept up the stairs to make their deliveries, and they seemed unaware of the cleaners who paid some of the female residents for sex to fund their drug habits.

I was living in a squat with a psychotic member of the Hell's Angels fraternity called Bradley when I was offered a place in this outwardly desirable hostel. I knew that if he got to know I was leaving he was likely to apply force to prevent me from going. So I tiptoed around, discreetly trying to pack my hairdryer and a few clothes into a small bag.

'I'm going out, Bradley. I'll do a couple of punters, score for us and be back within the hour.'

'All right, Angel, off you go, but hurry back sharpish, I'm clucking.'

Like everyone else in crack house circles he called me Angel. Very few people knew that my real name was Rhea. The conversation with Bradley was a repeat of one we'd had hundreds of times before. In the past I'd faithfully trotted back to him with the promised drugs and so there was no reason for him to doubt me this time. I edged out of the front door sideways so that he wouldn't notice my bulging bag, closed the door carefully behind me and then ran down the street as fast as I could. It felt like playing truant from school; exhilaration tinged with the fear of getting caught.

As I walked through the front door of the hostel, unpleasant feelings of being the new girl flooded back to me. It was like joining a school three years after the other children had started there. I recognised most of the people I saw walking around the hallway as fellow visitors to the local crack houses and smiled nervously at them.

'Hiya, Angel, welcome to The Ritz,' a couple of them quipped unoriginally. I gave them a watery smile.

I was ushered into a side room by one of the staff, a bored-looking young man in his early twenties. He slopped a cup of tea down on the table for me and dropped a pile of papers on top of the puddle the tea had made.

'Just fill those in, love, and then I'll show you to your room.'

The forms were complicated and mostly seemed to be for the benefit of the hostel to claim housing benefit on my behalf. I scribbled the answers quickly. I was desperate to get into my own room. It would be the first time in years that I'd had four walls and a door with a lock on it to call my own.

I was given room 133, easy to remember because it was the same number as the bus I often caught. When Bored Man unlocked the door I was expecting to see a cosy little space, neutrally furnished but comfortable enough to move straight into. Instead I saw the same hepatitis-skin-coloured walls as in the hallway, an institutionalised iron bedstead, a dull mattress, a scuffed wooden chair, chest of drawers and wardrobe and nothing else. A luminous yellow sharps bin to place used needles in sat on top of the chest of drawers. The staff obviously presumed that every resident injected drugs. I was terribly disappointed. It was cleaner than the crack houses I'd stayed in recently but just as bereft of warmth or any sort of humanising decor.

I nodded wordless thanks to Bored Man, closed and locked the door from the inside, lay down on the scratchy mattress and cried. I felt that the room represented the sum total of my life – bare, empty nothingness. When my sobs had subsided to a whimper or two, I heard a knock on the door. I had a bottle of water in my bag and splashed some of it on to my eyes to hide the fact that I'd been crying. Then I opened the door a couple of inches, thinking it might be Bored Man telling me I had failed to tick one of the interminable boxes on the forms. A slight, small woman was standing at the door with a broad grin that seemed to fill up most of her pinched face. Her brown hair was tied into a neat ponytail and she looked immaculate in a red T-shirt and jeans.

'Hi, I'm Miriam, your new next-door neighbour, welcome. Would you like to come in for a cup of tea? You can't have had a chance to sort your room out yet.'

'Sounds great, thanks,' I said. I picked up my key and carefully locked my door to protect my small, bedraggled bag of possessions. The turning of the key in the lock and the slippery shiny feel of it in my hand was a delicious novelty.

It was as if an entire universe rather than a flimsy brick wall separated Miriam's room from mine. Her room was decorated in frilly, girlie pinks – pastel chintzy curtains, fluffy sugared-almond pink rug on the floor, floral pink duvet cover hiding the ugly iron bedstead. The room smelt faintly of lavender.

'Come on in and make yourself at home.' She patted the bed next to her, the only proper place to sit in the room. On a wall bracket Miriam had a small colour TV mounted. Daytime TV played wordlessly as we chatted. Piles of equally frilly cushions were scattered across the bed. I dreamed of making my room look exactly like hers. Drug users have homing devices for each other. I always thought I concealed my drug use well but instead of putting the kettle on Miriam took two unused needles out of a small metal box and unwrapped a sludge of brown powder.

'Do you fix?' she asked, beaming. I smiled back. At that moment our friendship was cemented. Like me, Miriam funded her habit by selling sex. We agreed to go out to work together that night but a few hours later, when we had earned enough to buy our drugs and walked to the nearest crack house to buy them, I couldn't face the thought of returning to my cold, bare room.

'I'm going to sleep in the crack house tonight,' I said to Miriam. 'I'll be back in the morning.'

'OK, babe, I'll see you soon.' She winked at me. I felt cast adrift from my usual lifelines, the dealers, the corner shops that would buy secondhand goods from me, the people who lived nearby. But the sense of loss and dislocation was thankfully temporary.

It didn't take me long to settle into hostel life. They say that even in conditions of extreme adversity – prisons, concentration camps and the like – enterprise finds a way of existing. That was true of hostel life too. Becoming firm friends with Miriam helped enormously. We became accomplices at beating the system. We went down to breakfast wearing full make-up with our handbags slung casually over our shoulders. We helped ourselves discreetly to huge piles of toast, sandwiched two pieces together with butter and jam then dropped most of them into carefully opened serviettes sitting in our bags. That way we had enough calories to keep us going for the rest of the day if we found we didn't have enough money to buy food later on. I still worried about being too fat even though I could squeeze into a size six sequinned mini skirt that I used to stand on the streets in. But I always ate breakfast fearing that if I didn't I would become so hungry later on in the day that I might end up doing something heinous like gorging myself on a chocolate bar.

One of the ways Miriam and I deluded ourselves about our true, sorry state was to make hostile and superior comments about other addicts as we sat taking dainty bites out of our buttered toast.

'Look at the state of her,' I whispered to Miriam as a young woman with matted hair and enormous black bags under her eyes made worse by smudged mascara walked in.

'She's really let herself go,' Miriam muttered in agreement.

Any non-drug user who walked into the dining room would have said exactly the same about us but in the homogenous world of addicts Miriam and I decided that we were near as dammit at the top of the pile.

The breakfast conversations between the residents were monosyllabic, monochrome exchanges.

'Have you seen so and so? Tell them to knock on my door because they owe me money.'

There was also a moral hierarchy among hostel dwellers with regard to income-generating activities. Those who sat cross-legged on the street and begged for drug money for hours on end were scorned by the rest of us. If you wanted to hold your head up high at the breakfast table, it was important to work for your money. Shoplifting was seen as acceptable, as was fraud or prostitution, but begging was certainly not.

However cataclysmic world events were outside of the hostel, they rarely penetrated the crumbling Edwardian facade. The cycle of generating income to buy drugs, arranging delivery of the drugs, smoking or injecting the drugs and then dealing with the after-effects of the drugs was something which took up every waking moment of our lives. There simply wasn't time to think about, let alone to discuss, the concerns and preoccupations of the 'straight world'. My drug use escalated while I was in the hostel and I believe this was true of some of the other residents too. When my life was in orbit around one crack house or another I had to keep my wits about me in order to survive. Those survival needs generally put some sort of a brake on my drug use. But cushioned by the hostel, which would always be there providing food and shelter, there was no need to apply the same brakes. There was more scope to use drugs without any sort of responsibility rearing its head and so that's what most of us did.

I joined the working girls, as prostitutes referred to themselves, in selling sex to the hostel cleaners. It was wonderful to have regular customers that I didn't even need to leave my room to find.

21. A MOTHER RESUSCITATED

Some people love drugs, use copious amounts for a while but carry on with their lives, paying their electricity bills on time, holding down a job and engaging with their community. Others amongst us use drugs to the point of oblivion all day every day, and never want the experience of blotting out the self to end. There is a major difference between the first group and the second group. The first group tends to be reasonably contented with their existence and able to face the ups and downs that the world flings in their path. The second group is not. I of course was in the second, among the self-medicators fleeing pain of some description. Pain caused either by external events or by internal hopelessness. The drugs transform many of us into ruthless, selfish people who rob and prostitute ourselves through the days and nights because returning to the chemical stupor we urgently need to climb into is far more important than any pain or suffering we may cause others. However, at the point of embarkation on the drugs journey, members of this second group are disproportionately fragile creatures, too sensitive, perhaps, for the world.

It was the highly developed sense of negativity about myself that held me back each time I thought about getting in touch with my mother. It had been almost a year since we'd spoken. I felt terribly guilty. Each time I thought about picking up the phone I was filled with terror about hearing the hurt in her voice because I had abandoned her for so long. But once I was settled into the hostel my resolve stiffened and I decided to get in contact with my mother again. She was often in my mind but as is generally the way with people who surrender every waking moment to the frantic cycle of pursuit, ingestion, enjoyment and loathing of addictive drugs, she was jammed into the boxroom in my brain. For me addiction was like swimming round and round a glass-walled aquarium. Inside the tank was everything needed to sustain the drug habit – dealers, needles, crack pipes and various unpleasant means of generating income to purchase the said drugs. Outside it, sight and sound blurred and muffled by the glass and the water, was the rest of the world. Often it was too painful to look at the fuzzy images of loved ones distraught about the path we had chosen. Far easier to swish away from the glass walls and head towards the interior of the aquarium where drugs and kindred spirits were most strongly concentrated.

It was Mother's Day 2003 when I first picked up the phone to her. Miriam and I were feeling morose about the bedraggled state of our relationships with our families.

'I'm going to call my mother,' I announced to Miriam, sounding far more confident than I felt. It was a long time since I'd contacted her and I imagined that she was wondering whether I was alive or dead. The rest of the family wanted nothing to do with me, fearful that if I crossed their threshold I would rob them of every last penny. I like to think that enough of my morality remained for me not to do that to the people I loved, but had I walked into my brother's or my grandmother's house and seen a few £10 notes lying on the table I know it would have been too hard to resist stuffing one into my pocket – half a punter less, I probably would have said to myself to justify such shameful behaviour. My family knew that both to protect themselves from me and to protect me from the baser side of my drug-addled nature, they had to turn their backs on me. My mother, however, always wanted to maintain contact with me. Trembling, I dialled her number.

'Hello, Mum, it's Rhea here.'

I paused, praying that she would respond in the way I wanted her to. She did.

'Rhea, darling, it's so great to hear from you,' she said. I could hear joy and relief in her voice. There were no recriminations; she stayed calm and made it clear how happy she was to hear from me.

'Are you OK?'

'Yes, I'm fine, Mum, I'm living in a hostel in south London. At least I've got a proper roof over my head now and they feed us a hearty breakfast every morning. How have you been?'

'Yes, OK. Funnily enough I'm coming up to London in an hour or two. Would you have any time to meet up for a cup of tea?'

'Sure, why not? There's a fish and chip shop which isn't too far from Waterloo station. It's called Burt's Chippy and it's usually fairly quiet. Should we meet there at 7 p.m.?'

'Fine, see you later.'

'See you later.'

Both of us were trying to be nonchalant about the fact that we were going to be seeing each other for the first time in months. I imagined that underneath her calm, measured tone, my mother was as apprehensive as I was.

We met at the appointed time in Burt's, a cafe where grease deposits from the fryers made the walls, floors and red formica tables tacky to the touch. We ordered two mugs of steaming tea. Burt only did very strong or super-strong tea so we winced as we sipped. I assured my mother that I was well although I admitted that I was using a lot of drugs.

'How are you making your money to pay for all these drugs you're taking?' asked my mother tentatively, her brow furrowing.

'I go out working.' She looked puzzled. 'You know, on the streets.'

My mother put her hand over her mouth but managed to regain her composure quickly. She bent over and fumbled in her bag for her purse. She looked as if she was trying very hard not to cry.

'How much do you need to earn tonight to keep you, you know, going?'

'Well, I can't stop until I've earned at least £30,' I said, feeling terribly manipulative.

'I'm really sorry, mum, but I'm going to have to go because I've started to withdraw and if I don't have some more drugs I'll get very sick.'

She nodded understandingly although she looked as if she was about to burst into tears at any moment. I hugged her goodbye and we agreed to meet up again soon. To my eternal shame I still went out to work that night and used my mother's money for crack treats as well as my essential heroin top-up.

A few months after I got back in touch with my mother I also resumed contact with my grandmother, for whom I had always felt great affection. I had seen her regularly throughout my childhood and during the period when I disappeared I often wondered how she was. Rather late in life my grandmother had become an independent woman. She had a circle of female friends whom she went on outings and energetic hiking trips with. She found my descent into addiction baffling. Our first meeting was strained. She disapproved of the way I'd been living my life and said little. As time went by and I became more stable our relationship improved and I felt able to talk freely to her as I had when I was a child. I had last seen her around the same time as I had seen my mother, before I disappeared from view just under a year before. I was overjoyed to see her beloved, familiar face again. She still went to great lengths to set her hair and, apart from a few extra wrinkles, didn't seem any different to me from the way I remembered her as a child.

Getting back in touch with my mother and grandmother felt good. It was so comforting to see them again that I could no longer understand why I'd left it so long.

The next time I saw my mother, she turned up unexpectedly at the hostel. It was a very bad moment. Miriam and I and another young woman who loved speedballing as much as we did had all gathered in my room and were halfway through the ritual of preparing our drugs for injection when a member of staff knocked and announced through the door that my mother had arrived to visit me.

All three of us looked at each other, appalled. My sense of anticipation at the imminent injection of crack and heroin was at its height. I could taste the drugs on my tongue and my saliva had gone into overdrive in expectation of the chemical release to come. In the moments before I took my drugs I felt as if a huge tsunami of pain and problems was rushing towards me. There was only one way to head it off. For as long as I used drugs, staring the problems in the eye was never an option. The more a person uses drugs, the more problems accumulate and the more likely it is that that person will continue to use drugs to shut off these problems.

If I ever walked home from a crack house or from a night full of punters during the morning rush hour when people were heading purposefully to work or mothers were clutching their children's hands as they shepherded them through school gates, my self-esteem took an extra battering. I wanted to be in that club but knew I had failed when I'd tried. The only solution was to stop thinking about all that by taking drugs.

'Take her into my room,' said Miriam, 'and we'll save your drugs for you for when she's gone.'

I wasn't at all happy about that. I knew what happened to the best intentions of drug users to save other people's drugs for them; they ended up being injected into their near-collapsed veins.

I went downstairs and tried to look pleased to see my mother. But all I could think about was a way to inject my drugs without her seeing before Miriam and her friend gobbled them up. I was starting to get pains in my legs; always the first sign of withdrawal for me.

I took my mother into Miriam's room and put the kettle on to make her a cup of tea. I kept darting in and out of my room to make sure that my drugs were still there. In the end, unable to bear it any longer, I grabbed the loaded syringe from the table and ran back into Miriam's room with it concealed in the palm of my hand.

'Turn your back,' I demanded of my mother.

'What are you talking about, Rhea?' she said.

'Mum, I'm sorry, I'm withdrawing. I've got to inject myself or I'll get very sick.'

She turned away with a sigh, which I knew wasn't irritated but distraught. She leaned forward, elbow on her knee and chin cupped in her hand. I knew that I was causing her an unspeakable amount of pain but as ever the drugs came first. Afterwards I just lay there, silent and half asleep, not even attempting to feign interest in what she was saying. My mother exercised great self-restraint and said nothing. She told me later how enormously distressing it was for her to see me chemically nodding off in front of her with bits of blood all over the place. It was a world away from her own youthful experimentation with cannabis and a few hallucinogenics. Drug users mete out extraordinarily large dollops of cruelty to their families.

22. SUGAR DADDY

Around this time my luck improved. I acquired a sugar daddy. I didn't know that he was a sugar daddy at first. I was pacing the streets in the early hours of a very chilly February morning a few weeks after I arrived at the hostel. I urgently needed money to stop me from withdrawing. I had already started to feel as if I was coming down with a nasty dose of flu. And there was a big hole deep inside me which no human being, no material comfort, only heroin could fill. It was 2 a.m. and there wasn't a single car on the road. I couldn't even hear a distant, comforting hum of traffic. The silence was pure and eerie. Suddenly a car appeared. I was startled as I hadn't heard it approach. It made me think that it had been parked somewhere nearby, observing me. The car drove past me two or three times and then stopped. I felt like a vulture's prey, first circled then pounced upon.

I had been hoping the car wouldn't stop; the blacked-out windows and sense of being stalked made me nervous. But at the same time I was so desperate for money that I knew I would have to climb into the mysterious car if an invitation was forthcoming.

The driver wound the window down. He was an extremely well spoken man. He had the kind of perfectly enunciated English accent confined to graduates of Eton and a select handful of other public schools.

'Hello, do you want to get in?' he said softly. Shivering, I agreed. My instincts told me that he wasn't dangerous and I prayed I was right. I climbed into the front passenger seat and he started driving.

'What's your name?' he asked in an even, neutral voice.

'They call me Angel,' I replied.

'Angel, why's that?'

'A crack dealer christened me Angel. He said that with my white blonde hair and radiant smile I looked too unearthly to be caught up in the nasty, murky world of drugs and prostitution.'

The man smiled. 'He's probably right. The name suits you perfectly.'

'What's your name?'

'I'm George.'

'What do you do, George?'

'I run my own business. Import, export, you know.'

We chatted in an aimless, pleasant way for a few more minutes and then he parked the car and suggested we climb into the back seat. I started fumbling with his trouser zip as I presumed that was what was expected of me but there was no reaction in his face or his crotch.

'You don't need to worry about that,' he said. 'It's not sex I'm after but company. Because of my work I'm away for most of the time. But when I'm back in London I get terribly lonely. I'd like to meet up with you when I'm here, spend some time with you. You seem like a nice young lady and I'm sure we'd get along famously. Take my phone number and call me in a week or two.'

He took £20 out of his wallet, the going rate for sex, and then took out another £15 that he said was my tip. I couldn't believe my luck. A charming, well spoken man wanted to pay me to chat to him. He dropped me off close to the hostel, gave me a chaste kiss on the cheek and a brief wave and said he hoped we could see each other next time he was in London.

We began to meet regularly. True to his word he did seem more interested in conversation than in sex. As well as paying for my drugs and Miriam's too, the money George gave me helped me turn my room from a bare cell into a homely hideout. Within weeks my room looked as lived-in as Miriam's, with comfortable cushions and drapes in rich shades of plum and burgundy concealing the hepatitis walls and unfriendly floorboards. He also started taking me to Marks & Spencer's and buying me brand new clothes. It was years since the clothes I wore hadn't been secondhand or donated. The things he picked out for me weren't to my taste – flat, boring blouses and skirts – and I wondered if it was all part of what I suspected was his mission to transform me and mould me into the woman he decided I could be.

It was still freezing cold. Miriam and I took to huddling together in her bed, surrounded by little bags of chocolate buttons and Cheesy Wotsits, drinking endless cups of tea, while we watched daytime TV. We'd often been up for most of the night, so we lined up our heroin nightcap, and then post-injection, with wads of tissue stuffed in our groins to stop the blood from flowing, drifted off into a deep and peaceful sleep with Lorraine Kelly chirping in the background. I sometimes wondered if Lorraine was aware that her audience was so much more diverse than the housewives who formed the bulk of her viewers. For me this was the purest form of happiness I'd experienced for a long time.

George and I continued to see each other and my life became increasingly comfortable. Although he knew that I was a drug-addicted prostitute and I knew he was paying me to spend time with him, we kept up the pretence of a relationship for quite a while. He took me to restaurants and gave me money to buy food to take back to the hostel with me.

He was keen for me to stop using street drugs and after a while I told him that I had managed to give up illegal drugs and was now maintained on a methadone prescription. It wasn't true but I felt that the boundaries of the relationship were shifting and that little by little he was becoming more controlling. If I kicked against the things he wanted me to do I knew I would lose him and that would have been catastrophic. Inevitably we started to have sex – the first time was on his office floor. It didn't feel any different from sex with any other punter even though I had had a 'courtship' with him first. I felt that at that moment I lost what little remaining power I had over him. He knew more and more about me although I knew very little about him. He was divorced and travelled a lot.

One night I went on a wild drugs binge. I had saved up a couple of hundred pounds of George's money and had some I had earned myself. I went from crack house to crack house guzzling drugs until I no longer knew where or who I was. The following day, my brain feeling as if it had been blasted to smithereens and was now hanging limply off the insides of my skull, I met up with George. Instantly he went into accusatory mode.

'I know what you were doing last night,' he said grimly. 'You were crawling from crack house to crack house. I'm very disappointed in you.' I started to protest that I'd been at the hostel all night watching TV with Miriam but he placed his hand over my mouth.

'No more lies,' he said so quietly he was almost whispering. His tone made me start shivering uncontrollably with fear. Ignoring my distress at being found out, he began to reel off the address of every crack house I'd visited and the name of every dealer I'd bought drugs off.

I was appalled and impressed. Some of the crack houses were brand new ones which not many people knew about. He even knew the names of all the dealers. I couldn't understand how he could possibly have known those details unless he was either some kind of psychic medium or a private detective.

He continued catching me out but despite my lies and deceptions he still seemed drawn to me. One evening when I was out with him, I told him I had to leave early as I had an appointment with a drugs counsellor the next day. In fact, I needed to go out and work on the streets to earn some extra money. George had a house in Hertfordshire and I assumed that that was where he'd go after he dropped me off. I waited for half an hour and then jumped on a night bus from the hostel to my usual street beat twenty minutes away. The street was as deathly silent as the first night I'd met George. Suddenly I was dazzled by headlights. At first I couldn't see either the car or its occupants but after a few seconds cold horror slid down my body. It was George; he had caught me out again.

He wound down the window and said in that same chilled whisper, 'I knew it,' and drove off.

I felt as if all the blood had drained out of my body, because George was at least my partial blood supply. I started to think fast of a reason why I would be hanging around on the streets so late at night other than to pull in a punter. I decided upon a tale and dialled his number.

In between sobs, I said, pretty convincingly I thought, 'It's not what you think, George, really it isn't. It's Miriam. I can't find her anywhere and I'm worried she may be hurt.'

He sighed. He obviously didn't believe me.

'I'll talk to you in the morning, Angel, not right now.' And he put the phone down. We didn't speak the following morning and in fact I never saw him again.

This was a significant financial setback for me but despite it my world inside the hostel was becoming increasingly secure. Along with two cleaners, there was a little old man who lived at the hostel who also paid for my services. I was amazed that a frail man of his age still took such an active interest in sex and still had the physical ability to get an erection. I supposed it was all tied up with the survival instinct, which is programmed into us all right up until the end. The final piece of my punter jigsaw was another old man called Amal. He was Somalian and rhythmically chewed his way through little mounds of the stimulant khat every day. As a result he had trouble sleeping and used me as a human sleeping pill.

'You calm me down, Angel,' he always said. He lived a few doors away from the hostel. The convenience of having four regular punters on tap made up for my distaste at servicing them. The more energetically I thrashed around with them the quicker they were and the sooner I could get back to my increasingly womblike room at the hostel where Miriam, heroin, the Cheesy Wotsits and Lorraine Kelly beckoned.

23. HOTEL HOLLOWAY

It was ironic that as I entered this period of stability I was arrested and sent to jail for the first time in my life. A few months before, I had picked up a hastily abandoned carrier bag containing stolen cheque books and cards in a crack house. I hadn't decided what I was going to do with it and as I walked away from the house, looking rather worse for wear, a young and thorough police officer, his bulbous nose crimson with cold, stopped and searched me.

'What's all this, then?' he said, peering into the carrier bag.

'Oh, Officer, I found it at the bus stop and was on my way to hand it in at the police station,' I said, trying to sound credible and coherent and respectful. My efforts failed. I sounded like the slurred drug addict I was. He took me down to the police station. I wasn't charged with any offence but I was bailed to return at a later date.

I deliberately pushed this to the back of my mind and the date I was supposed to report back to the police station came and went. As part of my decision to become more stable I got myself a script for the heroin substitute methadone. Methadone didn't provide the same buzz as heroin but it had a two-fold appeal. Firstly, if taken regularly it prevented withdrawal and secondly it didn't preclude people like me from using as many street drugs as we wanted to on top of it. Of course, the idea behind prescribing methadone is to stabilise addicts and break the link with illicit drugs. For some it works and for others it doesn't.

I received my first script from a special clinic. It was handwritten. I hadn't realised that I was supposed to take it to a particular pharmacy and so I took it into my local branch of Boots. Because it was handwritten and came from a clinic the pharmacist wasn't familiar with he became suspicious that it was a fake and called the police, much to my consternation. The police ran a check on my name and the failure to appear at the police station in connection with the bag of stolen cheque books came up. I was arrested even though the police and the pharmacist managed to verify that the methadone script was genuine.

I was held in a police cell overnight. I was withdrawing and spent the night shivering and aching. I appeared in court the next morning charged with attempted deception and a few related charges which my pained brain couldn't process. I was still dressed in my street clothes – an exceedingly short skirt, knee-length black boots, a tiny denim jacket and a tinier strap top. My bleached blonde hair was up in bunches and the heavy black eye make-up I was wearing had smudged and pouched into streaks under my eyes. Needless to say the magistrate refused me bail.

I was taken down to the court cells and made to wait several hours. My achey shivers intensified. Withdrawing heightened my fear of setting foot inside a prison for the first time in my life. I had heard stories of female prisoners holding newcomers down and raping them with broom handles, of creative forms of bullying too sophisticated for men to dream up and of ferocious beatings by both prisoners and guards. The pain and anxiety made me cry. The guard, a plump white woman from a private security firm dressed in the uniform of ribbed navy pullover and matching polyester trousers, looked at me sympathetically and touched my shoulder gently. She had a no-nonsense Yorkshire accent. Tight grey curls framed her face. On her sweater was a badge that said Mary Cole, security officer.

'First time, is it, love?' I nodded. 'Are you withdrawing? Don't worry, they'll put you straight on the detox wing and give you some medication.'

''Ere, Shirl,' she shouted across to the next cell. 'You're headed for Holloway, aren't you, love? Keep an eye on this lovely young lady, will you? It's her first time.'

'No problem, Mary,' shouted back a voice I presumed belonged to Shirl. 'Everything will be sweet.'

'Shirl's a regular,' confided Mary in a comforting whisper. 'She'll make sure you're well looked after.'

Nothing happens fast in the plodding, monolithic police/court/prison complex. And when you're withdrawing, time goes 400 times slower. Eventually we were placed in the prison wagon, claustrophobic self-contained booths with moulded metal seats. The smell of paraffin filled the van. I felt as if I was going to choke. There were high, tiny windows which I peered out of. We were travelling along the Embankment and I could see dozens of free people walking along, handbags and briefcases swinging jauntily. I had never envied people walking down the street before and of course had never appreciated my own ability to do so. But suddenly I ached for my liberty. Finally we arrived at HMP Holloway, a notorious women's prison where many women are placed before being dispersed elsewhere. The booking-in process was interminable; it probably took more than six hours altogether to complete the many different piles of paperwork. The whole business gave me a peculiar sensation, like trying to remain vertical on a floor which rocks from side to side, a sort of seasickness of the soul.

New arrivals are systematically stripped of a sense of their own identity. Clothes and shoes have to be handed in along with any other possessions. Once stripped (literally) of those things which make the being you display to the world different from that of the next person, you are reconstructed as a prison clone. I was handed a baggy maroon tracksuit. My beloved stiletto boots were immediately confiscated as a 'potential offensive weapon' and I was handed an ugly pair of HMP green slippers. Even the tobacco and Rizlas we were given had the HMP stamp on them. We were no longer creatures of the world. We had been consigned to a hidden world where the tracksuits and Rizlas and slippers veiled our identities from ourselves and others.

By the time I was shown to my cell it was nearly 10 p.m. and I felt terrible. A woman called Donna was my cellmate. She looked at me shivering pathetically.

'I guess you arrived too late to get your methadone,' she said. 'Don't worry, you should still be able to get something to make you feel better. How good is your acting?'

'Pretty lousy,' I said, momentarily forgetting my convincing performances in Soho, and as a prostitute pretending to like men I loathed.

'Well, do your best. What you have to do is lie on the floor and pretend you're having a fit. You know, you keep banging your head from side to side and jerking your body.'

That sounded like rather a tall order for a non-thespian like me, particularly as I was neck-deep in withdrawal, but I promised to try. I lay on the freezing cell floor and writhed rather unconvincingly.

'Nurse, nurse, come quick, my new cellmate's having a fit!' yelled Donna through the cell door. After a couple of minutes a stout, bored nurse came along, lifted the flap on the outside of the cell door to have a look at me, tutted disdainfully and walked off.

'If that girl's having a fit then I'm a banana,' she said scornfully. 'You ladies really should try something a little more original to get your drugs,' she added as her footsteps disappeared into the distance.

'Oh, well, never mind,' said my cellmate. 'It'll soon be morning and you'll get what you need then. When you go and see the doctor tell him you're a heavy drinker with a huge crack and heroin habit. That should cover all the bases and you'll get a hearty dose of methadone, Librium and Valium.'

I did as instructed and was given enough medication to keep me contented and pain-free. Once I no longer had withdrawal to contend with, I started to enjoy prison life. I became friendly with a woman in a cell across the landing. Donna showed me how a hand mirror and a makeshift sling could be used to signal a note was on its way and then to swing it through the door flap. The process involved writing a short note and then tying it to either a piece of string, a shoelace or a strip of sheet torn off the bed. The cell doors had a small flap in them which could be lifted to reveal the corridor outside. If there were no guards patrolling that stretch of corridor at that moment the first step was to flash a hand mirror through the flap to the cell opposite to get the cellmate's attention. Once the intended recipient of the note was on standby the note was duly swung through the flap on the piece of string. The whole thing had a touch of the Enid Blytons about it.

While most of the women weren't remotely religious, I discovered that it was de rigueur to acquire a rosary as a Holloway souvenir. I duly appeared before the prison chaplain, faked Catholicism and got my rosary.

After two weeks inside I was released. I was pleased yet disappointed too because I found the place quite comfortable and had made some good friends. My mother had been informed that I was in Holloway and had succeeded in getting bail for me. I ran out of the prison gates yelling: 'I'm free! I'm free!'

My mother was there to meet me at the gates. She hugged me and shushed me at the same moment.

'Keep your voice down, Rhea. What will people think?'

'Thanks for getting me out, Mum, I appreciate it,' I said.

She smiled. 'I hope this is the first and last time.' My mother was close to Keira and Paul and had remained in contact with them during the months of my disappearance. As she drove me back to the hostel she said: 'How would you feel about getting back in touch with the children again? I think that getting out of prison is a new start for you. They keep asking me when you'll be better and I keep telling them that you're on the mend.'

She didn't push me but her suggestion was just the opening I'd been looking for but didn't have the courage to initiate myself.

'Oh, mum, you know I want to see the kids again more than anything else in the world. If you could arrange a meeting that would be fantastic. Maybe I should see Paul by himself first. I imagine he knows what's been going on with my drug use in a way that Keira doesn't. I need to sit down with him and have a proper talk.'

My mother nodded and said she'd see what she could do. She dropped me back at the hostel and as soon as I'd waved her off I called my favourite dealer, a sweet-faced man called Kai. Whatever time of day or night I called him he was obligingly there for me with my order. Sometimes he looked as if he'd sleepwalked to wherever we'd agreed to meet. When I finally stopped using drugs, friends who were still using told me he was overjoyed for me.

'Tell her not to go ringing my phone no more,' he said and he really meant it. He was too good and too kind to be a dealer – and too careless. I heard a while ago that he'd been deported to Jamaica.

The day after I returned to the hostel my mother called me. 'I've had a chat with Paul and he's very keen to see you. How would it suit you to meet in Burt's café again at 4.30 p.m. tomorrow? That should give Paul time to get there after school.'

'That's great, mum. Thanks for playing go-between, it makes everything much easier for me.'

'Don't worry, Rhea, everything will work out fine,' said my mother.

We met the next day as arranged. Paul had grown a couple of inches since I'd last seen him almost a year ago. His hair was cropped just a couple of millimetres beyond his scalp. He was dressed in baggy jeans and a grey sweatshirt. I searched his face for his familiar, cheeky grin but he remained expressionless. He looked a tortured mixture of frightened and angry.

'Hello, Paul, how are you doing?' I asked softly. I was scared to hug him in case he pushed me away.

'Where have you been mum?' he said gruffly as the three of us sat at Burt's greasy formica table. My mother and I sipped tea while Paul drank Coke.

'I'm so sorry, Paul. I've been having a very rough time. I wouldn't have been able to look after you properly. I just wanted the best for you, to make sure you were well cared for until I could come back to you.'

'Don't think you can just walk in and out of my life whenever it suits you,' he said. The hurt in his voice gave me a pain in my head.

'I'm sorry, I don't know how many ways I can say it. I hate myself for leaving you but I just couldn't cope. I'm getting better now, though, and as soon as I can find a place for us to live you, me and Keira will be back together again as a family. And I promise, no more madness.'

Although Paul knew I used drugs he didn't say anything about my drug use to me. He'd found my crack pipe hidden under the floorboards before I handed him and Keira over to Darren and he said nothing on that occasion either. He was twelve then, very streetwise and knew I was up to no good.

I asked him some questions about school and about how it was working out living with Patrick, Jill and Tom. He had recently moved in with them because he wasn't happy staying with Darren's family.

His answers were monosyllabic but by the end of our meeting he had warmed a little to me. Once we were back in touch we met all the time. Paul became more communicative and tentatively began to trust me when I said I wasn't going anywhere. With Keira things were much easier. She was only six and all that mattered to her was having her mummy back again. The first time I saw her at Stella's house she bounded up to me, flung her arms around me and remained glued to my lap until it was time for me to leave. Holding my beautiful, trusting little girl in my arms again was one of the best feelings I'd ever experienced. I stroked the soft skin of her cheek and smoothed her plaited hair.

It took more than six months of increasingly frequent contact with my children before they really began to trust me again. I knew that there were no short cuts back and that the only way to show my love was to keep on turning up faithfully and regularly and never to say I'd be there for them at a certain time and then inexplicably fail to appear. After about six months of laying new foundations with them I began to see them both almost every day. The strength I got from seeing them and feeling their trust in me grow countered my guilt about having failed them. I was determined that this time I was going to succeed as a mother.

I went back to court seven months after I was released from Holloway and was given a two-year suspended sentence and a £300 fine. I was relieved to have escaped with nothing more than that. A prison sentence would have been an enormous setback despite the camaraderie and availability of prescription drugs inside.

When he presented his pre-sentencing report to the magistrate, my solicitor said that I was becoming more stable and had found myself a job in a hairdressing salon in Willesden Green. One of the conditions of getting bail was that I should straighten my life out, stop using drugs and get myself a job. My life was straighter, although not entirely straight, my drug use was more stable and by the skin of my teeth I had a job.

I was aware that people in the court were staring at a patch of hair above my forehead which I had dyed a fiery shade of red. I had dyed the rest of my hair back to its natural brown and was wearing a sober trouser suit. I was standing before the same female magistrate who had seen me stumble dishevelled from the cells seven months before. She seemed incredulous at the transformation in me and pleased with herself that she had given me a chance and I hadn't let her down.

'May I ask, Miss Coombs, what your employment is,' said the magistrate, leaning forward and pushing her slippery glasses further up the bridge of her nose.

'Hairdresser,' I said. A few people tittered.

'Ah, I did wonder,' she said, nodding in the direction of my hair.

'You're free to go, Miss Coombs. I wish you the very best of luck with your hairdressing venture and with making a go of your life.'

'Thank you.' I beamed and strode out into the sunshine.

24. SHAKY STEPS

As I started to fill my lungs with the fresh, pure air of normal life, my children helped pull me even further towards them. A chemical readjustment had taken place in my brain. The paralysis which had made me self-destruct appeared to be lifting. I could move my leaden limbs again and all I wanted to do was run as fast as I could, back to my children. Although guilt surged through me like a fast tide whether I was with them or apart from them, it didn't stop me from seeing them as often as I could.

Paul started turning up unannounced at the hostel. I was overjoyed to see him but utterly paranoid that he would discover the needles I stabbed my groin with or my crack pipe. All the equipment of my addiction was carefully hidden beneath a pile of clothes in the locker by my bed. But all the same I didn't want to let him into the hostel, populated as it was with dissolute people like myself. My delight at seeing him was tempered with a powerful sense that he was entering a tainted airspace which I didn't want to be any part of his life. I thought that just by inhaling the same oxygen as I had while injecting my drugs he would be contaminated in some way. Usually we met up outside the hostel and went off and had a cup of tea together or sat in the park and talked.

Thoughts of trying to give up drugs were sloshing around my brain, like a wine sampler who glugs the liquid from one side of their mouth to the other before gently spitting it out. The flavour wasn't too bad. It was so good being a mother again. Paul talked to me about mundane matters and it felt exciting.

'My teacher told me he liked the rap I put together. He said I showed talent and that if I worked at it I could get somewhere,' he told me. 'Mum, what do you think the chances are of me getting the Nike trainers that I totally, totally need?'

As far as I was concerned, these were words of love. Having tried to combine motherhood and chaotic drug use once before and failed, I knew realistically that I couldn't have both. The more I had of my children, the more I wanted them. Keira didn't visit me at the hostel but I visited her all the time at Stella's house.

I was thinking more clearly than I had done for years. I was approaching a kind of reckoning which often comes to drug users after being in an extended stupor for years or even decades; a realisation that there was no easy way out of this, only a hard way. The crack house lifestyle finally seemed to be losing its charm for me. One evening I was sitting in a particularly filthy and chaotic crack house when Sheila, a woman I knew, staggered in. Doctors assume that all afflictions which drug users present them with are symptoms of drug use. However, drug users generally know better. We become experts at spotting drug-related health problems and those which have nothing whatsoever to do with drugs. I took one look at Sheila and knew that she was seriously ill and that whatever was wrong with her was not caused by excessive speedballing. She was burning hot but shivered violently. She was clutching her chest.

'I can't breathe because it hurts too much,' she said. I wondered if she was having a heart attack. 'Come with me into the bathroom and have a pipe with me,' she pleaded.

'I'm sure that's the last thing you need at the moment,' I said.

'No, no, I know it will help me.' We locked ourselves in the bathroom and smoked some crack together. While crack house dealers are happy to sell heroin alongside crack, they don't like people injecting the stuff in crack houses in case they overdose and have to be taken away by ambulance, thus drawing unwanted attention towards the crack house. Sheila and I then made ourselves a small speedball each. By now the dealer was banging on the door for us to come out.

'No fixing in this crack house,' he yelled.

Sheila slumped on to the floor and I half carried her out on to the sofa.

'I must go out and work, I've got no money left,' she said in a weak, slurred voice.

'Don't be silly,' the assembled users chorused. 'You can't work on the streets in that state.' They looked at me. 'You off out to work, Angel? Don't worry, we'll make sure she gets to hospital.'

I was reassured and left the crack house to find some punters. I returned two hours later assuming that Sheila would be gone. But she was still slumped on the sofa semi-conscious while everyone smoked around her. It was as if a half-dead person wasn't on the sofa at all.

Although I had left her, I was enraged at everyone else's selfishness. They had promised me that they would take care of her and instead they looked away and carried on smoking.

'You fucking cunts!' I yelled. 'Look at the state of her – she's barely alive. I'm going to call an ambulance.'

I dialled 999 and told the operator we would wait by the roadside in front of the block of flats where the crack house was. That way the crack house wouldn't be identified.

I half walked, half carried Sheila down three flights of stairs. The pavements, cars and rooftops all had an icy frosting and every minute it felt as if the temperature was dropping further. I sat down on an icy bench and laid Sheila down, placing her head on my lap. Thankfully the ambulance arrived just a few minutes later, its siren blaring reassuringly. The paramedics took one look at Sheila and said, 'We need to be quick.'

They lifted her expertly on to a stretcher. She groaned softly. I sat and held her hand while the paramedic listened to her chest as the ambulance whizzed us to hospital.

'What do you think is wrong with her?' I asked.

'Sounds like she's very seriously ill with pneumonia, love,' said the paramedic kindly. 'Crack smoker, is she? That won't have helped her chest. Do you know what drugs she's taken? She won't get into any trouble but it's important that the doctors know.'

I hesitated for a moment then said, 'She's been smoking crack and injecting crack and heroin.'

'Righty-oh, thanks for telling me that, love. We'll be there in a jiffy and they'll probably get her straight on to IV antibiotics.' He looked at her arms. 'If they can find a vein, that is.'

I looked at Sheila lying in agony on the stretcher and felt sickened about our lives. I was scared that each laboured breath she took would be her last.

Once we arrived at the hospital, she revived slightly. She was rushed to the intensive care part of Casualty and the pneumonia diagnosis was confirmed. The doctor started grappling with first one of her forearms and then the other in a bid to get the IV antibiotics set up. He failed and became angry.

'Bloody junkies, what do they expect,' I heard him whispering under his breath.

Sheila hauled herself into a sitting position and lifted the hospital gown she'd been placed in to reveal her skinny, shrivelled groin.

'Why won't you listen to me? The only place left for a needle to go is into my groin.'

'I can't do that,' the doctor said. 'It's very dangerous and if you do it I take no responsibility.'

'I'm not asking you to fucking do it,' she said weakly. She grabbed the needle off the doctor and inserted it straight away. 'Satisfied?' She lay back on the pillow and closed her eyes as antibiotics flowed into her abused, papery veins.

The doctor visibly relaxed once he could see that the IV was properly set up.

'Thanks for bringing her in,' he said to me. 'You've saved her life. If you'd left it another couple of hours she probably wouldn't have made it.'

I went over to Sheila, who was either asleep or unconscious. She had more wires than limbs.

'Bye, babe,' I whispered to her, squeezing her hand. 'You take care.'

I decided to walk back to the hostel rather than getting the bus because I thought the clear, chilly night air might do me good. I had believed that those who congregated in crack houses were my surrogate family. We had laughed and joked and smoked as one. But suddenly all I could see in them and their artificial habitat was ugliness and moral squalor. A friend's life meant less to them than smoking the next rock and the next. I knew my own behaviour was not exactly unselfish but suddenly I decided I wanted no part in that lifestyle any longer.

Detox was periodically suggested to me. Before I had always dismissed the idea without giving it much thought but it was suggested again three months after I'd saved Sheila's life and, without allowing myself time to visualise the sweats, the aching bones and the scream from every cell to drip back in the drugs I was depriving them of, I said: 'Yes, I'll do it, but please can I do it now before I weaken?'

My experience with Sheila had made me more keenly aware than ever before of the fragility of human life. A couple of green shoots of responsibility suddenly poked themselves through my brain. The same brain which had propelled me towards self-destruction for so many years. My guilt about abandoning my children constantly gnawed at me. It was so bad that it felt as if it had chewed all the flesh off my bones. Yet now this new emotion, a yearning to live, had arrived. It tempered the guilt and filled me with a resolve that I could and would change.

The resolve was still rather shaky, though. For drug users, one world can be exchanged for another very quickly and once the switch has been made the new world becomes the whole world and loyalty to all previous worlds is wiped clean from the memory. That was how hostel life felt to me. Soho, crack houses, life with Darren were all forgotten. All I wanted to do was cling to the universe I had established at the hostel – my regular punters, Miriam, the thickly buttered breakfast toast which by now took less than a second to drop into the waiting serviettes in our handbags, the daytime TV routine. Suddenly all those things were very dear to me. I had just agreed to go to a strange place inhabited by strange people where my body and soul would be stripped of every chemical crutch and left stark naked to cope with life's cruel and harsh moments.

But it was too late. I'd said yes and if I backed out now I'd feel even more of a failure than I did already. Miriam was happy that I wanted to make changes in my life but at the same time she seemed hurt that I was abandoning her. I spent the hours leading up to my entry into detox in time-honoured fashion – taking as many drugs as I could physically cram into my body without killing myself, a narcotic last supper. I kept telling myself that I really did deserve this last treat.

I ordered a taxi to take me to the detox, which turned out to be a pleasant establishment not too far from the hostel. As the taxi drove through the wisteria-covered archway I could see people sitting out on the lawn in groups on white, plastic garden furniture. Mostly they looked gaunt but they seemed to be well past the immediate agonies of withdrawal and to be coping with the place, holding apparently normal conversations and even smiling or laughing now and again. I didn't catch sight of anyone sprinting past me through the archway towards freedom and decided that the whole business was probably manageable and that I really would make an effort to stop using drugs once and for all.

I was booked in and assigned a room. I still felt fine but as I looked at the four magnolia-painted walls I knew that in a matter of hours I would be screaming and begging to be released from them and would hate every brushstroke of bland paint.

I lay down and tried to sleep. Just as I was dozing off a nurse knocked on the door. She was warm and plump and smiley and had comforting grey brillo-pad hair. A million miles away from the drug users I consorted with, and presumably appointed to this job in the hope that her cosy, non-judgmental manner would offer a bridge back into the straight world.

'Hello, dear, I just need to take a few details from you to work out how we'll reduce your methadone.'

'OK, fine,' I gulped, praying that they'd accidentally forget to reduce it at all, so that even if I couldn't experience the pleasure of illicit drugs I wouldn't have to experience the pain of leaving all chemicals behind me.

'What's your methadone script and what sort of quantities of street drugs are you using on top of that, lovey?'

I swallowed hard again. Like people who surreptitiously increase the number of cream cakes and chocolate biscuits they eat but never actually count up the escalating total because it would be too shaming, I tried not to think about precisely how much crack and heroin I was tipping into my body. But I realised that there'd be no point in underestimating my true intake to the nurse as I'd only get less methadone.

'Well, I'm on about 65 mls of methadone a day and I'm using about £200 a day of crack and heroin on top of that,' I said, hanging my head.

'Mmm, well, we don't usually take people here unless they're on 50 mls of methadone a day or lower, but we'll let that pass and see how you get on if you're really determined to give detox a whirl.'

'Oh yes, I am, I am,' I said in a voice which sounded hollow and utterly devoid of conviction.

The nurse squeezed my hand and said, 'I'll pop back later. I'll have a word with the doctor about your dose.'

At first I didn't feel too bad but I was terrified of venturing out and making conversation with the other addicts. I felt too naked without my crack and heroin crutches.

The staff reduced my methadone very quickly and in what seemed like no time at all I was down to 3 mls a day. When that was taken away from me I felt pain and misery like none I'd ever experienced before – not when DP forced a detox on me in his crack house and not when I hadn't had enough money to buy heroin and so had started to withdraw. In the early stages of withdrawal I managed to snatch a few hours of sleep here and there but as my symptoms became worse my sleep tapered off to no more than a few minutes at a time. My withdrawal had begun with flu-like symptoms, which were unpleasant, but the agony accelerated quickly, like a car initially loitering in first gear then suddenly switching to fifth with the throttle changing from a purr to an angry spit. Everywhere was pain. It's hard to remember the taste of pain when you're not experiencing it but when you're locked inside it and there's no escape there's nothing worse. I had never noticed that my bones could emit pain before but now I writhed on the floor bashing my legs just to get the agony out of them. My bones had become an enemy invader and, delirious with withdrawal, I kept trying to think of a way to remove them. I started imagining having a collapsed face without a skull, with eyes lolling into the fleshy remainder of my nose and both dribbling towards my mouth; and my heart sagging towards my thighs, which contained only baggy flesh and skin. I didn't want to die but I wanted to burst out of my body, leaving it behind while the part of me made of nothingness floated away peacefully. But I stayed in my body and I survived.

After the acute phase, I bobbed around in a sea of bearable pain. I could make a cup of tea and even hold a conversation without wincing. Both acts felt as luxurious as dining on caviar off a golden platter. And then that pain passed too and I was left feeling cleansed as if the clearest stream water ran through my veins instead of blood.

But the sensation of renewal, of being physically and spiritually purged of chemicals, didn't last long. Soon I joined the others in detox's most popular pastime – plotting ways to smuggle drugs in. The building we were in backed on to a row of houses and it was announced – whether as a result of wistful conjecture or proven fact I never discovered – that a woman who lived in one of the houses was a local dealer. Some people did walk out of detox but those who stayed ultimately made little effort to send smoke signals over the fence to our neighbourhood dealer. Just talking about breaking the rules seemed enough for them.

'I'll order the biggest rock you ever saw and smoke it all in one go,' said one rather wan-looking girl with doleful eyes and hair bleached to the colour and texture of straw.

'I'll go straight back into my groin with the needle,' said a bearded man who longingly licked his lips.

One of the most terrifying things about detoxing from drugs is the way opiate-deadened emotion suddenly awakens and smacks you in the face with all the force of a juggernaut. Nobody felt like spilling out the pain of their childhoods, the failed love affairs, the chances missed, the friendships squandered. So instead we engaged in junkie small talk.

'How many times have you gone over?'

'How do you do your speedballs?'

'Have you come across Mad Johnny, the meanest dealer in the world? Always puts an extra piece of clingfilm over the crack so you can't see what you're getting.'

The others seemed sated by the talk but it only served to whet my appetite for the real thing beyond what I could physically endure.

'I'm leaving,' I announced to the kindly nurse a few days after I had completely detoxed. 'I can't take another minute in this place. I've no idea why I ever wanted to give up drugs. My life is fine with drugs. It's the people who don't have their passage through life eased by drugs that I feel sorry for. Life really is the biggest bitch and you have to do what you can to make it bearable.' I rambled on and even found myself repeating my old, dead friend Dave's saying that drugs wouldn't have been put on the earth if God didn't want us to enjoy them.

The nurse let me go on until I could think of no more justifications. I sat defeated with hot tears dripping into my lap.

'Why not just stay until after lunch, dear?' she said. 'You're experiencing a rush of emotions. In a few hours' time you may have entirely different thoughts forming in your mind.'

'No, my mind has never felt clearer and more focused,' I said. 'My destiny is drugs. I need to leave right now. Every extra second here is torture.'

I ran up to my room trembling with failure tempered by excitement and anticipation. I could already taste the smoke from the crack pipe in my mouth, and the familiar feeling of holding the syringe between my teeth while I readied my vein to receive a blissful heroin and cocaine cocktail. I called a taxi and within ten minutes it had arrived and swept me out through the wisteria-covered archway, back into the world.

What I hadn't realised was that I was terrified of being with my naked self and was instinctively running back to hide myself in my drug clothes. Later I learned that naked could be OK, that bad experiences didn't equal failure but an opportunity for growth. Later I would see a demand to pay a rent arrears bill of £33 as a manageable request for payment of £33 and not as a demand for £1 million which had to be paid immediately otherwise I would end up with my head chopped off. But not yet.

As soon as we were on the main road, I called my dealer.

'I'm out of detox. Can you get me ten of white and ten of brown as quick as you can. I'll meet you round the corner from the hostel.'

I sank back into my seat and sighed contentedly. Staff at the detox had begged me to go easy if I started injecting again as even a small amount of drugs could send my body into overdose. I injected half my usual dose and lay on my bed, enjoying the rush.

'Thank God,' I said, sinking back into my cushions.

25. THE END

But after those first moments of heady pleasure I became fidgety. It was getting towards my time. Many but not all drug users arrive at their 'time'. Some die first and some have the chemicals so tightly knotted into their DNA that their 'time' is strangled before it can arrive. Having announced to the world that I was going into detox, it was humiliating to return, head hanging low, to the sex workers' clinic to pick up clean needles and condoms once again. I thought of the friends I had made in detox who would have moved on to the wholesome rehab by the sea by now. My drug appetite was waning; I no longer had the energy for mad binges and sold just enough sex to earn £40 for a day's drugs. Many drug users who want to stop using have a series of false starts before they succeed and I was one of them.

I had a few brief periods of abstinence at the hostel. I was prescribed Subutex, a drug which blocks the effects of opiates, and for a while I used only that. I put a notice on the door of my room in clear, deliberate green felt-tip. It read: 'Please do not bring drugs to my room or offer any or ask me to get them for you. My room is a drug-free zone. I don't take drugs any more. Thank you.' To my surprise and faint disappointment, all the other hostel residents respected my request. Paul still came to visit me frequently, which I loved, and I started to spend a lot of time at Stella's house. I adored sitting in her warm, welcoming house, my hands cupped round a steaming mug of coffee. Most important of all to me was the fact that she didn't judge me.

'Listen up good, honey. We none of us perfect but we're all God's creatures. It's not for any of us to stand in judgement over one another, that's the job of the Good Lord. My door is always open to you no matter what happens, don't you forget that. As far as I'm concerned you're my daughter and I'll always love you.' She wrapped her arms around me and squeezed tight.

'Thank you, Stella, you don't know how much that means to me. It means a lot, really.' As I became more stable, I spent every day at Stella's. Keira loved having me sitting waiting at Stella's big kitchen table when she came home from school.

'Mummy, Mummy, I'm so glad you're here.' She flung her arms around me, giving me the same rapturous greeting every day. By the time she was getting ready for bed I was desperate to leave because my craving for my next fix of heroin was becoming too overpowering.

'I'm so sorry, darling, but if I don't get back to the hostel to sign in by a certain time I lose my bed for the night.' It was a lie, of course, and it only served to intensify my guilt about leaving her. She cried inconsolably every night and Stella had to peel her little fingers off my neck one by one and scoop her up into her arms to try to soothe her. I skulked off to my dealer, hating myself more than I thought it possible to hate.

But despite inching my way back towards the world people who didn't take drugs inhabited, the street was still part of my life. I felt comfortable, safe and accepted there. I rarely worked in the daytime. It made me feel too exposed, like a Dracula-figure withering in dazzling sunshine. Daylight was for the 'normal' people and the night belonged to us, the misfits from the straight world. I knew the foxes, the night bus drivers, the drunks; all the creatures of the night who moved noiselessly side by side, rarely brushing against each other because there was so much more space in the night than in the day. The world of daytime had chewed me up and spat me out but in the community of the night I could be anything I wanted to be. I wasn't shunned by the night creatures; they merely blinked uncritically at me and moved on. The street meant different things to me than it did to day people. When I looked at dustbin cupboards at the front of estates I wondered whether they contained women like me allowing themselves to be furtively, urgently screwed for £20 or less; when I peered down poorly lit side streets I didn't feel fear, only interest in the place as a future venue to rendezvous with a punter; when I saw a bus stop with a sign for night bus 137 it was more welcoming than a lighthouse in a bad storm at sea. Night buses were ghostly, empty things with drivers who seemed so transparent against the black sky they almost weren't at the wheel at all. The night buses carried me back to the hostel, to warmth and away from punters for a few hours. I really, truly loved the night bus.

I had held on to my hairdressing job at the salon in Willesden Green.

I felt a bit of a fraud trimming hair and recommending styling products to customers. I was pretending to be a straight person like all the other hairdressers, but really I was like Eve after she had bitten into the apple dangling from the Tree of Knowledge, while the rest of them had not yet tasted the fruit and perhaps never would.

I had found a way to circumvent the blocking effects of the Subutex I had been prescribed. After a brief break from heroin when I was first prescribed Subutex, I went back to it. I continued taking the Subutex with the heroin and also continued to smoke crack. I started falling asleep while doing highlights, and while I was shampooing, my head would suddenly loll forward and my wrist would droop, spraying soapy water into the client's eyes.

The manager, Marilyn, was a kind woman who worked and worked to make her salon a success. After a few months I decided I had to leave before I really disgraced myself and betrayed her trust in me.

'I'm so sorry, Marilyn, but I'm having a few problems with my children at the moment and I'm going to have to leave and try and sort out some better childcare before I can think about taking on another full-time job.'

She looked at me curiously then said, 'Thank God it's only that. I thought you had a smack habit.' I vigorously shook my head, trying not to blush, and wondered if she had spotted the signs because she had been in that situation herself once. I never got to find out. She paid me up until the end of the week and I left at the end of the day.

Although I was delighted to be reunited with heroin and crack when I left detox I was becoming disenchanted with the drugs again. I maintained my contact with Paul and Keira but could once again feel things spiralling out of control. I continued taking the Subutex but it had become almost an irrelevance as I injected more and more heroin and crack.

Deep in gloom, I was offered new accommodation in Whitechapel, a part of London I had never lived in before, where I knew no dealers and had no idea which street corner the desperate, withdrawing prostitutes stood on. I decided it was a sign that the time had come once and for all to clean up. I resolved to have a long goodbye to drugs and went on a forty-eight-hour binge. As I packed my suitcases I smoked and injected and smoked and injected and packed a T-shirt or a pair of knickers once every hour or two. A van had been booked to transport me and my possessions from south to east London but when it arrived

I locked myself in the bathroom so that I could inject myself one last time. Then I threw all my remaining needles into the yellow sharps bin and ran outside to the van. I hugged the women who were my friends, the ones I had stood on the street with, sat in crack houses with and shared fixes with. I didn't hug them too long or hard, though, in case I turned around and ran back inside the hostel.

When the van driver had carried my things into my flat, I felt too tired to unpack anything. I fell straight into a heavy sleep on the bare mattress of my new home. When I woke up the next morning I was withdrawing. I wandered out into the street in a shivery daze looking for human signs of drug use. I stumbled into a couple of teenagers who looked glazed and wasted. It felt horrible not knowing where to go or who to call.

'Excuse me,' I said hesitantly to the girls. There was a flash of recognition in their eyes as they looked me, a fellow desperado, up and down. 'Do you know where I could score?'

'Walk this way, darlin',' said one of them, a coarse-skinned, harsh-voiced white girl who looked no more than nineteen. She and her friend led me down a warren of back streets. Pungent curry spices hung in the air. The dealer was an Asian man, which startled me. I had only ever seen black dealers in south London and it hadn't occurred to me that the ethnic background of dealers changed according to whichever group was most economically disadvantaged in a particular area. I had no needles or any other injecting equipment and ended up sharing the single rusty needle the girls had with them – something I had rarely done before for fear of contracting HIV or hepatitis C. My withdrawal symptoms vanished but I was sick of the pursuit of drugs and the afterpain of using drugs. Before I'd left the hostel, I'd been given the address of a twelve-step fellowship meeting in Covent Garden. I decided that I'd try it; anything was better than chasing lousy drugs into nowhere.

I arrived at the building where the meeting was being held. It was a dusty church hall with bare floorboards and notices up about times of services. Everything inside the church was brown. I had never been religious but I felt uneasy stepping inside the house of God to talk about my worship of white rocks and brown powder. I stood in the doorway trying to scent the mood of the place like a dog sniffing out a newcomer. I decided the whole thing seemed too hard and that I would retreat and try to find a dealer. Since I had arrived in Whitechapel I had felt more lost and alone than I could ever remember feeling since my childhood. The combination of being in an unfamiliar area with my usual lifelines and familiarities stripped away and knowing that the last syringeful of heroin that I had injected into my body was fading fast was too much to bear. No reasonable person would expect me to cope with such a double whammy of adversity, I argued with myself. I turned round and was about to walk away when a man and a woman approached me. I could tell immediately that they were not using drugs. They looked clean and wholesome. But I also sensed from the look in their eyes that they had a history and had not always looked and felt so presentable.

'Coming to the meeting?' the woman asked gently. She had ivory skin tinged pink by the cold, long brown curls and a kind face that didn't judge me. She was wearing a dark wool coat and had a soft lilac scarf around her neck. I neither nodded nor shook my head. Perhaps the woman had once stood hesitantly in the doorway in exactly the same way I was doing now. 'Come on in with us, we'll look after you. These meetings really are good. We couldn't get through the day without them, could we, Des?' She turned to her male companion who beamed and nodded. I felt simultaneously trapped and relieved to be trapped as I followed the couple inside the building.

In that first meeting I sat on a hard chair in a circle with twenty other people and just listened. People spoke of their experiences of drug using, their struggles with sobriety and ultimately the belief in themselves and the 'higher power' which allowed them to maintain their abstinence. It was all very alien to me and yet familiar too. Although the people in the room were from all ages and backgrounds and had had wildly varying drug-taking careers I experienced a sense of coming home. 'This is where I belong,' I thought to myself. I'd had an identical sensation at previous junctures in my life – when I started rebelling at school, when I dropped out of school and smoked cannabis all day long in the St Paul's area of Bristol, when I first started working in Soho, when I became established in DP's crack house. Yet something different was happening here. On all the previous occasions, when I had felt a sense of belonging I was moving further and further away from society in order to feel at ease inside my head. Now for the first time I was taking a step back towards the community I had shunned. But instead of feeling revolted and ill at ease I could for the first time in years see that there was a space for me inside the social order. My self-imposed exile to the nether regions could be over if I wanted it to be. I had a sensation of being crammed inside a dim cardboard box and being able to uncurl a little because a few stray shafts of light had suddenly pierced the gloom. These flashes of light were feelings, long-dormant emotions not atrophied by drugs. And they weren't feelings of unbridled pain but of pleasure and joy. Before, the fleeting sense of belonging had come from my actions, but now what was going on was happening entirely inside my head. At last I heard the click. It suddenly dawned on me that I had been waiting thirty years to feel like this.

What I felt in that room was unselfish love. It was a long time since I'd experienced that. I was held inside people's kindness as if I had been strapped into a gentle safety harness and was no longer spilling out all over the floor. I hadn't felt this when I was in detox but now for the first time giving up drugs seemed not only desirable but perfectly possible. After the meeting I almost skipped home. I had unloaded a terrible burden in the meeting room and now was light and unencumbered. I was also very tired. I lay down on my bed and fell into a deep sleep.

I woke up the next morning sweating and shivering as the final dregs of heroin leached out of my bones into thin air. I had just £3 left. Part of me wanted to go and stand on the street, hoping to flag down a passing dealer and ask if he could sell me three tenths of a wrap of heroin, but I was too weak to move off the hard blue sofa, which was standard issue with the flat. There's a very specific smell that withdrawing addicts have: a dank, rotting smell that comes out in their sweat in little droplets of death. For the first time I was beaten by drugs. I huddled into the corner of the sofa, curled into a tight little ball as if trying to burrow my way back into my mother's womb. I was dressed in an oversized hooded grey jacket and an old pair of jeans which hung pathetically off my skinny frame. For thirty seconds the clothes couldn't keep me warm enough then I'd suddenly be drenched in sweat and want to strip them off.

Somehow I found the strength to call Denise, the worker at Spires who had given me so much support. 'Please, please, could you come? I've got nothing. I'm clucking. I can't do it, I can't go on.' I let the phone drop and prayed that she would come to me.

She jumped straight into her car, children in tow, and helped me more than she can ever know.

'Come on, Angel, you can do this, you've done it before. At least it isn't methadone this time, which is such a bugger to come off.' She held me and mopped my forehead and forced sips of water and tea down my throat. And she was right. Once again I came through the other side of drugs. Inside me I felt it was the last time and it was.

26. KINDNESS

Throughout my final withdrawal I knew that I had hit a brick wall. There was simply nowhere else to go. I had had my fill of feeling disappointed in myself. I was tired of letting myself down. For the next few months I clung on to the fellowship meetings for dear life, attending two or three a day. They were the only thing standing between me and the void. I didn't want to go backwards into the world of drugs but wasn't yet ready to go forwards and move into the world of sober usefulness. The meetings were a criss crossing of supportive hands laid across the deep canyon between drugs life and no-drugs life. Stepping across it was a slow and treacherous business but I was determined to inch my way forwards. I only managed faltering baby steps but I didn't fall over and I didn't turn back. At the meetings, being surrounded by people who were enthusiastic and who were willing to change what was defective about their lives was a wonderful salve.

I went to many different meetings in many different church halls and community centres and although the faces and the colour of the walls changed I always got the same feeling of being supportively held, like a baby in a sturdy pair of mother's arms. The people I met seemed both normal and happy. They wore nice clothes from high street stores and could afford to buy a whole packet of cigarettes at once rather than cadging individual cigarettes from dealers and non-drug users.

Slowly my self-esteem began to plump out like a thirsty, withered plant watered at long last. It was a pleasant, unfamiliar feeling. The others sensed how fragile I was in the beginning and were extra careful with me. For the first time I felt as if I was precious and that nobody wanted me to break. In the world of crack houses it is assumed that everyone is made of Tupperware and can be bounced up and down endlessly. The less resilient do of course break but everyone else shrugs and moves on to the next rock. There's no time or space for sentimentality in a crack house.

I was terrified of being alone and so it seems were some of the more established twelve-steppers. They invited me to go for coffee with them after meetings. There was the familiarity of being with addict kindred spirits yet the peculiarity that none of us were scurrying off to score.

'What do you fancy, Rhea, latte, cappuccino, mocha, hot chocolate?' asked the woman I'd met on the first day with the brown, curly hair. Her name was Millie. I hadn't spent much time in coffee shops over the last decade and I wasn't sure what to choose.

'I'll have whatever you're having,' I said, trying to sound coffee confident.

A few of us sat holding steaming lattes.

'How're you finding things, Rhea?' asked Millie.

'Pretty good, I never thought I'd be able to get as far as I have without drugs. The world isn't actually as terrifying as I remember it being before I started using.'

'It's the same for all of us,' said Millie, flashing a big, open smile. 'So much of what happens in life is down to your internal assessment of yourself. If you think you'll never be able to live without drugs, or go to university or sustain a relationship or be a responsible mother, then that's what happens. But once you realise that all those things and more are perfectly achievable, everything changes.'

If a drug worker who had never experienced addiction had said those things to me I would have been inclined to dismiss them as platitudes. But coming from Millie, who told me she used to have a £400 a day crack and heroin habit and lied, stole and had sex for money to fund it, I believed every word.

Millie had had a good job working for a fashionable art gallery in Chelsea. Cocaine was freely available and her glamorous recreational habit soon exploded into unglamorous addiction.

In the twelve-step meetings I sat in Millie and the others all found different ways of expressing the same thing – a hole inside them, a mismatch with the world, a sense of being apart from everyone else. This sense of isolation and incompleteness, I realised, is as much a part of the human condition as having two arms and two legs. What was key was the way we tried to fill up that chasm between how we felt and our perception of which way contentment lay. Perhaps if I had known that many others felt more or less as I did and that my feelings weren't some kind of emotional freak show I wouldn't have spent so long wandering hopelessly down a series of blind alleys.

'Everyone has those feelings,' said Des, the man Millie had been with on the first day. He was a studious-looking black man who always carried a pile of literary novels under his arm.

'I've just been reading some Albert Camus. He felt a lot of the same things we feel, only he sat down and wrote some bloody great books about his thoughts and feelings. Maybe you should try writing, it can be very therapeutic.'

I pondered on what he had said and after we said our goodbyes and I was walking back to my flat I stopped off at a newsagent and bought a large spiral-bound notebook with a mottled fuschia cover and one of those pens which write with thick, wet ink, making every word look shiny.

There was so much I wanted to write, about love, addiction, isolation, despair. I'd never tried writing before but the words flowed easily, as if they were perched on the edge of my brain waiting to be let out. This was one of my first attempts.

SEVEN DAYS

Trying to get it right,
Is harder than you think.
Wake up in the middle of the night,
Just before I sink.
Have to go on the pavement,
I hope it won't take too long
To profit from your investment,
Singing that same old song,
And I know how it will be,
When I walk through the door
Hoping they won't see me.
But I can never be sure.
If the bell rings on the way out
Someone will have something to say.
And if I don't hear them shout
Then this could be the day.
What I have in the bag
Should take away the pain.
Day to day it's such a drag
To know I will have to do it all again.
No I don't want you looking.
So much better on my own.
I know how to keep it cooking.
Got more numbers than I can phone.
Now I'm back where I don't belong
Ain't no way to live.

They want to make me wrong.
Never enough what I give.
Feeling warm and satisfied
How long will it last
In myself, where I hide
To chase away the past?

I was proud of my efforts. 'Not bad for a first timer who dropped out of school,' I said to myself. Writing was another new, unfamiliar pleasure and so was praising myself for something I'd achieved.

In the early stages of my recovery I exchanged the self-absorption that had circled around procuring, ingesting and recovering from drug taking for a fascination with the way I could function without drugs. But after a while the novelty of poring over every particle of the new, sober me wore off. I still attended twelve-step meetings daily. If the taste for heroin and crack implanted itself particularly deeply in my brain, I attended two or three meetings a day. I was often tempted to use drugs again, fantasised about the sense of homecoming I would experience if I could just smoke one tiny rock of crack or pierce just one of my recovering veins so that my body could be stroked by heroin one last time. But the part of me that wanted to be drug-free triumphed over the part that didn't. I resisted temptation. Experts say people use drugs to run away from the reality of painful issues in their lives. That is undoubtedly true and I was one of those doing that for years, but drugs also provide a magnificent buzz and they become as much a part of you as a precious but troublesome member of the family. When I eventually stopped using drugs I felt that I'd lost that difficult, beloved person. In the end, though, I hated what drugs made me more than I loved the drugs and I started to hate myself even more than I did before I started taking them. To this day, thinking about drugs gives me a simultaneous flutter of euphoria and a sickness in the pit of my stomach.

As the distance between me and drugs increased I started to notice the world beyond me. I listened to the news now and again, paid attention to the non-drug woes of the new friends I had made on the twelve-step programme, listened to them talking about struggling to pay their bills or visiting an ailing parent or planting some daffodils in their garden. I never could have imagined that such mundane talk could be so pleasing. I began writing to-do lists and at the end of each day everything I'd written on my list had been crossed off with a flourish. When I was using drugs I rarely managed to do anything beyond using and scoring. The control I had over my life was a delicious novelty.

The further away I moved from my drug use the clearer my mind became. While I had been using drugs and selling sex I had pushed thoughts of HIV or hepatitis C infection to the back of my mind. I had been quite careful but not 100 per cent careful. In times of desperation I had shared needles and as my relationship with my sugar daddy George became more established I had agreed to stop using condoms with him. I was certain that by the law of averages I would have contracted at least one of these two life-threatening viruses. I resolved to get tested, booked appointments for a blood test at a local clinic, then chickened out two or three times. In the end, though, I knew that I couldn't put it off any longer. I sat in a chair at the clinic and extended my arm to the nurse. My damaged veins had healed enough for her to take blood.

'Try not to worry too much, dear,' she said looking at my anxious face when she'd finished labelling the test tube. 'You'll get the results soon enough and then at least you'll know.'

The following week I contacted the clinic. I nurtured a glimmer of hope because nobody had contacted me. I thought that if the news was bad I'd get a phone call asking me to come in and 'discuss the results'. But my phone remained silent.

'Oh, hello, it's Rhea Coombs here,' I said nervously. 'I'm phoning about my test results.'

I could hear the receptionist shuffling papers and tutting as my results eluded her. Eventually she found them.

'Ah, yes, here we are: Coombs Rhea, HIV negative, hepatitis C negative.'

I burst into tears of shock and relief.

'Thank you, thank you, thank you,' I sobbed, feeling an enormous debt of gratitude to the receptionist, as if she'd personally arranged to keep the two viruses away from my body.

'Congratulations, that's excellent news,' said the receptionist. 'Make sure you continue to have protected sex, though, won't you?'

'Oh yes, of course,' I said. That receptionist had no idea quite how excellent the news was, given my previous lifestyle. Once again I had had a lucky escape. I had survived against the odds. 'I'm supposed to survive, I'm meant to be here, there's a reason for all this after all,' I whispered to myself after I'd put the phone down, euphoria spreading through my veins in a warm mist.

The news that I was HIV- and hepatitis C-free gave me a huge boost and I was making enormous strides with putting my life back together but of course things weren't perfect. Without drugs I began to put weight on, something which worried me enormously. I began taking laxatives to offset the effects of having no crack to whirr the calories to a pulp in my stomach. I also began to take an unhealthy interest in websites that celebrated anorexia and bulimia and offered tips about ways to pretend to be eating in front of other people without actually swallowing any food. After a while I managed to wean myself off laxatives and made an effort to eat regular, healthy meals as a way of warding off fresh bouts of my eating disorder. I remain insanely jealous of women who are naturally slim and can eat whatever they like without gaining a pound, but I feel that my eating disorder is now under control, although it rears its head in times of stress. I eat for my children, for myself and in order to hang on to my job.

During my healing period I sat on the bus and watched junkies through the window, hurrying purposefully down the street to meet their dealer, limping because they had abscesses in their legs so bad they were in danger of losing them. I had met one woman when I was living in DP's crack house who was only able to bear the pain of the abscess in her leg because of the daily dose of methadone she took topped up with heroin. A drugs worker had stopped her in the street when he saw that she was obviously in a lot of pain and could barely walk.

'What's up, Sarah? Don't tell me you still haven't been to get that abscess treated yet. Let me take a look. Roll up your trouser leg,' he said.

Sarah winced and complied. The drugs worker was so shocked he almost jumped backwards. She had shown him a festering mass of yellow and green pus that was literally eating her leg away like a swarm of bees guzzling a honey jackpot.

'Sarah, if you don't get to A&E now you're going to lose that leg.'

'I can't spend hours hanging around in A&E because I'll start withdrawing. I have to go and get my daily juice [the slang word for methadone] to get myself out of trouble. Then we'll see about A&E.' She winced and hobbled off. Many drug users who needed emergency medical attention refused to go to hospital because while waiting in A&E, sometimes for several hours, they don't receive methadone to stop them withdrawing, until or unless they're admitted to a ward. A&E staff say that if they gave methadone out in A&E they would have hundreds of reasonably healthy junkies queuing round the block with imaginary complaints just so they could get a dose of methadone.

I saw Sarah a few weeks later and the diagnosis of the drugs worker turned out to be right – she had indeed lost her leg below the knee. She seemed unperturbed.

'I'm doing all right on me crutches, probably better off without that damn leg, it was troubling me so much,' she said matter-of-factly. 'When I couldn't take the pain any longer I got myself to hospital and they chopped it off for me. Ever so quick they were.'

As I watched the shuffling addicts out of the bus window I thought of Sarah and knew that, incredible though it sounds, at one point if I had had to choose between keeping my leg or withdrawing I would have cried: 'Take the leg but give me my drugs.'

27. A SPACE IN THE WORLD

Paul and Keira were of course the two people who kept me focused. Paul was living with temporary foster parents while Keira remained with Stella. I spent more and more time with them, helping them with their homework, buying them new bits of their school uniform and listening to them chatter about who had dissed who that day amongst their peer group, who was in and who was out of the in crowd and what food they wanted me to cook for them. A social worker came and assessed me in my little flat in Whitechapel and nodded approval that as I seemed to be 'moving forwards' Paul could come back to me. It had been more than a year since we'd lived under the same roof and I was excited but terribly apprehensive about Paul's return. My flat had only one bedroom and the social worker said that until I could be rehoused in a bigger place Keira would have to remain with Stella.

When Paul came back things between us felt perfectly natural. I continued to feel ashamed about how I had let him down but there had always been a close bond between us from the time when he was a baby, the time when we escaped from Billy, the years I had stood in his primary school playground waiting for him to bound out of school, determined that I would never, ever be late.

Although we never discussed my drug use in detail Paul knew what I had been doing. It seemed enough for him that I was back in one piece and could be called on to hand over cash, my phone and anything else I had that interested him. In the last few years he had never talked much about his feelings but as each day passed I could see that he was becoming less watchful and more relaxed in my company. Like most teenagers he took the view that I was there to service him. In other circumstances I might have reprimanded him for his cheekiness but I silently celebrated the fact that he felt relaxed enough with me to treat me that way. I was simply 'mum' and that felt good. We argued about his wayward behaviour when he ran around the streets with his friends and at times I could see that he was angry with me for dipping in and out of his life like a flickering flare. But still I knew he was glad I was back and in the end that was all that mattered.

Denise remained a loyal friend. Like my twelve-step friends she kept on encouraging me that the things I wanted to do I could do.

'I'd love to go to college and train to be a drugs worker and learn how to counsel people. I feel I'd know what to say to them,' I said to Denise one evening when we were sitting in my flat sipping tea, a lousy sitcom on TV turned down in the background, making the wooden actors look even worse as they mouthed their lines. 'But I didn't exactly excel myself at school and I've hardly got any qualifications.'

I'd never been able to see the point of anything I'd learnt at school but suddenly I understood that abstract subjects could have relevance to surviving and succeeding at life.

'Look, you can do it if you want to,' said Denise. 'Why not enroll on the drug worker course I did at the local college and see how it goes?'

I also had a drug worker from my time in the hostel who, like Denise, kept on encouraging me. I nervously enrolled on a drug worker's course and a counselling course for the 2004/5 academic year. Both were part-time, one-year courses so I could study for them at the same time.

To my amazement I loved being there. My mind opened outwards like the petals of a flower catching raindrops. I soaked up everything I was taught and was even enthusiastic about the homework.

'If only I'd felt like this about learning when I was at school I could have been a brain surgeon by now,' I joked with Denise.

Most of the other students had never used drugs in any significant way and I was keen to play down my own extensive experience. I didn't want to be continually associated with my past, nor did I want to appear like a know-it-all whenever we were asked technical questions by our tutor.

One of our assignments was to make a crack pipe and prepare some imaginary heroin for a hit. I was very apprehensive about doing that. I was trying so hard to leave my past behind and wondered if the act of preparation – such a vital part of the ritual of drug use – would act as a trigger for me.

'Don't be ridiculous,' I said sternly to myself. 'You're in the middle of a college classroom and your teacher has asked you to do something, just get on with it.'

So I did, calmly and competently. I hadn't forgotten what to do and finished my preparations quickly and deftly. I had been so immersed in what I was doing that I hadn't noticed what was happening around me. I looked up and could see pandemonium. All the students who had never used drugs were struggling to get things right, and they were panicking because the teacher had given us a certain amount of time to finish the job off.

The scene reminded me of a crack house full of wild-eyed junkies desperately trying to get their needles and crack pipes in order because they simply couldn't wait another minute or two for their hit. I grinned broadly. I was very far away from that place. I could fashion a crack pipe out of a little glass bottle, get a syringe ready for injection and it all meant nothing to me. No cravings were triggered off inside my head, no yearning to return to the life I had struggled to leave behind. I had truly moved on.

My counselling course taught me many things: how to trust my instincts, how to express myself without inhibitions. If I was going to help others to do that, I had to learn how to do it myself. I passed both with flying colours and glowed. It was the first time I had succeeded academically. It seemed natural to return to Spires, the place which had helped me so much, to ask if I could now help them.

'Come in, come in,' said the manager, beaming. 'It's great to see you, Rhea, and we're all delighted you've done so well. We don't have any job vacancies at the moment and often we like people to start off by volunteering and see how it goes. How would you feel about that?'

'Yes, that would be great, perfect. I'd love to volunteer here.'

'Of course all your expenses will be paid.'

At first it felt peculiar to see the men I'd sat on battered sofas in crack houses with and the women I'd stood on the street with, sometimes companionably, sometimes competitively, depending on how desperate we were on a particular night.

They seemed to find it less strange than me.

'Well done, Angel, you've made it out of the hellhole, we're so proud of you.'

Some of the women hugged me tight. There wasn't a trace of resentment amongst them that I'd succeeded while they continued to fail.

At first I identified more closely with them than with the other members of staff but that soon changed. I was taught about professional boundaries and I learnt fast.

'We're very pleased with your work, Rhea,' my manager said to me after I'd been volunteering for six weeks. I was thrilled and told her that I would love to be considered for a paid job if one came up. When I'd worked as a hairdresser my aim had purely been to earn enough money to support myself and the children. But this was something different. I wasn't driven by money but by a need to repay the things I knew I had taken from society. For the first time in my life there was a chance that instead of being known for doing wild, dangerous or anti-social things I might be known for doing good work and helping people in need. The staff were very supportive of me and never minded however many questions I asked them. In January 2006 I was offered a part-time job at Spires.

'Would you like to join the staff here?' my manager asked with a smile. I felt so good about myself to have secured this on merit. People I respected actually wanted me for what I could offer to some of the neediest and most vulnerable members of society.

Of course there are many good workers who support this group who have never experienced the lifestyle themselves. But I felt that my experiences had served as a long and painful apprenticeship to getting this job.

I knew the tricks that addicts played, the lies they told to themselves, the blind alleys, false starts and endless disappointments. When I talked to the clients we used our own private shorthand. I knew what they were thinking because I had thought it too. I hoped that remembering the selfish, wasted me who moved, slurred, between street and crack house on a very short piece of string and seeing the stable responsible me I had become would give those who wanted to change a little more belief in themselves.

At the end of each day I tidied my desk and straightened my phone. Did I really deserve my own personal desk and phone, both of which had become central to my new identity as a woman with a responsible job, I sometimes wondered. I'd been given a three-bedroomed house by my local council and Keira was spending more and more time with me. Her father Darren adored her and told her she was his 'princess' all the time. Although Darren and I were no longer together I felt that she was getting a lot of love from both her parents.

I walked to the supermarket to buy a chicken to roast for dinner – Paul's favourite – and followed three or four other mothers also struggling with shopping bags on to the bus. It was raining hard and a film of passengers' breath and water which had dripped into the bus steamed the windows. The other travellers looked tired, annoyed with the rain and the traffic and anxious to hurry off the bus. But I couldn't stop smiling. I rejoiced in the thoughts of my children, my job and my home. That day I had nagged and cajoled to get a desperate woman with a heavy crack and heroin habit into a detox programme. The administrator on the phone kept telling me she'd have to wait at least two weeks but I knew that in two weeks' time she would be lost. If she had any chance she needed to go now, 999-style, before her resolve faded. In the end the administrator agreed. I put her in a taxi and wished her good luck.

She had hugged me and said: 'You've helped me more than you can ever know,' the same words I'd said to Denise when I was at a similar point. The symmetry of it pleased me enormously. I had tried to show her love in the professional sense and to convince her that I believed in her, because that's what people who had strayed from society needed more than anything else. I leant back against the rough fabric of the bus seat and closed my eyes. Now the discordant components of me fitted together into one person. My soul felt untroubled, at peace. There was a purpose to me being put on the earth after all and perhaps without the crazed, wretched years I never would have discovered it. At last I had found my place.

EPILOGUE

I wouldn't recommend the experiences I have been through but they have undoubtedly made me the woman I am today. I had been in a terrible rush to be an adult but once I had gazed into the world of adults I wanted to run away screaming back into my childhood. I couldn't lose face and do that, so instead I chose the mask of drugs. They allowed me to be nominally present in the world of adults while emotionally I ran somewhere far away.

On my many journeys hurtling towards self-destruction, I picked up some invaluable survival skills. Without them I wouldn't be who I am today. In my twenties I careered towards disaster, meeting it more than halfway. But now I have developed a different instinct. I can often pre-empt a bad situation and I have the sense to walk away. Looking at addicts, particularly those in their twenties, from the position of newly confirmed outsider status, so many of them appear to be having an extended bout of the terrible twos. Since I had reinvented myself in my early teens, I had always had a reputation as a tough person. I realised that people were often fearful of me and

I was pleased. It meant that my layer of insulation between the raw, hurt me and the world was working well. The new post-drugs me emerged gradually, like a snail taking tentative steps out of its shell. Each real-world task that I achieved meant that a little more of my old skin had been shed. I had to smash up the old me until it was completely destroyed before a fresh human being could emerge from the ashes of the old, hopelessly addicted me with barely a functioning vein in my body. To an outsider I must have appeared a fearless person, consorting with gangsters and taking vast quantities of drugs. I wasn't scared of any of the things that many other people are frightened of, but unlike many other people I was scared of myself and ran as far away from that self as I could possibly go.

These days I walk down the street and observe people. Before, my eyes were cast perpetually downwards while my mind fixated on my many failings. Now I think about myself far less because I have finally started to connect to the world. I have realised that the world never did deliberately shut me out but that I shut myself out. Everyone has a right to belong to the world – it isn't an exclusive club – but entry requirements are a belief that you have a right to belong.

I know that as I sit in my dark coat, jeans and trainers, people are unlikely to guess what my life was before. Then I look at them, decide what they are and where they've been in life, then rein in my assumptions and think that there could be as much of a mismatch between their appearance and what went on before in their lives as there is with me. And I like that. It makes me feel that nothing is really decided or finite, that everything is uncertain, in flux, and that that's the way it's meant to be.

Although the prostitution damaged me I don't regret that either. I have begun to understand that you can learn more from the bad experiences than from the good ones. I hope that people who read about what happened to me might look at a woman they see shivering on a street corner differently. Even if people aren't able to smile at another human being who's vulnerable, not scowling would be a start. Most of the women walking up and down the streets on freezing cold nights are homeless. None of us planned a career in prostitution and a variety of dire circumstances in our lives forced us to converge at the same desolate spot underneath the rest of society. A kind smile can keep us warm for a little while but staring right through us as if we don't exist is equivalent to felling us with an axe. Prostitutes don't damage society. Where damage is done it's done to ourselves. Women who work on the streets to support an expensive drug habit don't choose prostitution. It is simply the only option left to them. Crack and heroin are their pimp.

Women who sell sex in flats, saunas or brothels rarely use Class A drugs and have different economic reasons for involving themselves in this work. Some of us are more profoundly affected than others as a result of systematically scissoring our legs open and closed for money. But what is certain is that any woman who finds herself involved in prostitution out of one desperate economic necessity or another has a right to be safe and protected and to have realistic exit routes out of prostitution. Whether she is dragged kicking and screaming by a ruthless trafficker into a suburban massage parlour or chooses to work ten hours a week in a brothel because she earns the same as for a forty-hour stint in a call centre and can spend more time with her children that way. De-criminalising prostitution would increase the safety of the most vulnerable group – women working on the streets. Endlessly charging women with soliciting, placing them before the courts and fining them so that they have to go straight back out to work on the streets to pay off the fines makes no sense. It makes even less sense serving them with anti-social behaviour orders which, if breached, can lead to a jail term. Yet soliciting, the main offence committed by women working on the streets, is a non-imprisonable offence.

Women don't deserve to be killed horribly by warped men because they work as prostitutes. Sanitising the street scene by clearing prostitute women away puts them in greater danger. It means that they are forced to tout for business in darker, more remote areas where punters who are minded to can slit their throats with impunity. Designated areas away from people's homes with health services on board could help protect women who find themselves in this situation. Genuine (rather than token) support services to help women leave prostitution, repair the emotional damage in their lives, help them leave drugs behind and gain the skills to secure alternative employment would protect them even more.

Often I still feel that I don't deserve good things but I'm learning to accept that perhaps I do. One of my biggest post-drug pleasures is confronting things which frighten me – bills and work and difficult emotional situations – and managing them very well. Instead of hiding under the wave and choking on the sea water I'm riding on top of the wave that hurtles towards the shore. I'm far more intuitive now than I ever was before. I never allowed myself to trust my instincts but now that I do I've found that they often guide me in the right direction. The drugs I used to take made me paranoid and depressed. I spent a lot of time crying when I was under the influence although I often didn't know what I was crying about, so disengaged was I from my undrugged emotions. I still have moments when I feel low but they pass. I know now that feeling down doesn't automatically equal failure. I have learnt to follow the curve of doleful feelings in the certainty that they will pass. Before, the drugs were the equivalent of having a hand clamped over my mouth so that these feelings couldn't breathe or speak.

All I want now is to carry on giving something back, to shorten the long journey back to a normal life that I took myself on. I feel in a position to suggest a few short cuts, to erect signposts for those who want them. Although I understand better than most the women on the treadmill who stand shivering with their thin clothes wrapped around their scraggy bodies, no human being can change another unless they themselves want to change. It's always easy to judge, to say that if we had been made of sterner stuff we would have resisted the dissolute temptations placed in our path and performed our duties towards ourselves and our children more robustly. For those who have never struggled with light and dark, such remarks are cheap and effortless. If it was easy, everyone would be doing it. The dealers would be queuing up for unemployment benefit and the punters would be prowling empty streets.

Of course it isn't manageable for everyone and that's why so many women find themselves knotted up with things they would give anything to become disentangled from. Like me, the women I know ended up on the streets as a way of taking themselves out of a world they found too painful to inhabit. These women grapple with quicksand and often they give up and sink. Whether they end up in the situation I was in through DNA, circumstance or the random series of events which make up our lives, they need to be loved and supported and understood if any sort of change is going to come.

And as for Paul, now sixteen and Keira, now nine, being back for them, watching them grow and learn about the world, is a pleasure that a mother who has never lost her children, however fleetingly, cannot understand. Without them, who knows whether I'd still be in the crack house quagmire.

I go clothes shopping with Keira, I relax at home with them after I've cooked us all a meal and I talk properly to Paul, whom I went through so much with and who probably knows me better than anyone on earth. Every second of withdrawal, every bad night, every moment I failed was worth it in the end because it led me back to my children.

I know that I've hurt them and my mother on my journey to stability and I hope they can forgive me. I also know my children sometimes worry that I'll vanish again. I keep assuring them that I'm here to stay and truly I am. I've tried out so many bad things in life and after many detours rejected them. I love my children more than anything else and now that I've discovered that life can be good, I want to help them discover that too.